JOHN QUINC
GAG RULE, 1835–18

JOHN QUINCY ADAMS AND THE GAG RULE 1835–1850

PETER CHARLES HOFFER

UNIVERSITY OF GEORGIA, ATHENS

Johns Hopkins University Press | *Baltimore*

The Johns Hopkins University Press
2715 North Charles Street
Baltimore, Maryland 21218-4363
www.press.jhu.edu

Library of Congress Cataloging-in-Publication Data
Names: Hoffer, Peter Charles, 1944– author.
Title: John Quincy Adams and the gag rule, 1835–1850 / Peter Charles Hoffer.
Description: Baltimore : Johns Hopkins University Press, 2017. | Series:
   Witness to history | Includes bibliographical references and index.
Identifiers: LCCN 2017008835| ISBN 9781421423876 (hardback : alk. paper) |
   ISBN 9781421423883 (paperback : alk. paper) | ISBN 9781421423890
   (electronic)
Subjects: LCSH: Adams, John Quincy, 1767–1848. | United States.
   Congress—Rules and practice—History—19th century. | Antislavery
   movements—United States—History—19th century. | Freedom of
   speech—United States. | United States—History—Civil War,
   1861–1865—Causes. | United States—Politics and government—1815–1861. |
   BISAC: HISTORY / United States / Civil War Period (1850–1877). | SOCIAL
   SCIENCE / Slavery. | HISTORY / United States / State & Local / Middle
   Atlantic (DC, DE, MD, NJ, NY, PA).
Classification: LCC E377 .H75 2017 | DDC 973.5/5092 [B]—dc23
   LC record available at https://lccn.loc.gov/2017008835

A catalog record for this book is available from the British Library.

Special discounts are available for bulk purchases of this book. For more information,
please contact Special Sales at 410-516-6936 or specialsales@press.jhu.edu.

Johns Hopkins University Press uses environmentally friendly book materials,
including recycled text paper that is composed of at least 30 percent post-consumer
waste, whenever possible.

CONTENTS

PREFACE

In this series, the authors try to bring history alive by taking readers back to a time and place to see and hear events the way people then saw the world. The rewards of re-creating the past are especially rich in political history, for it is all about people in public life facing real problems. The aim is to see the political figures and hear their words as if they were in front of us.

The subject of the present book, the gag-rule debates in Congress in 1835–50, returns readers to Washington DC in the period before the Civil War. Then, the capital was still a southern city, with slaves walking the streets and slave traders conducting their auctions on the steps of public "slave pens" in sight on the Capitol. A member of Congress could not make his way from his boardinghouse or hotel to the chambers of Congress without being reminded that half the nation was slave country. It was against this blot on the nation's image that the abolitionists began their petition campaign. The issues in the congressional debates over the reception of antislavery petitions in the antebellum period may seem transparent, but the language the participants used had deeper connotations than a casual reading reveals. The purpose of this volume is to place those debates in the context of a nation divided by the slavery issue.

Imagining oneself sitting in the galleries of the House and Senate, listening to the speeches of what arguably was the greatest generation of political orators, is exhilarating. The debates themselves (unlike today's C-SPAN coverage of largely empty congressional chambers) were the height of political drama. When John Quincy Adams, John C. Calhoun, Henry Clay, and Daniel Webster, among others, rose to speak, a hush fell over the packed houses. Newspaper reporters sat alongside visitors in the galleries or in the aisles, taking notes as fast as they could, hoping to get them into print that night for their morning paper's readers. One could hear the national political process at work and sense the vitality, the danger, and the passions of the politicians, when so much depended on their words.

The signs and symbols of slavery still surround us in statues and buildings honoring the defenders of slavery. These dot college campuses across the land. A book on the effort to still the voices of antislavery advocates in Congress is not just a book about the past; it is vital reading for students.

A last word or two: There are, in the concluding portions of this book, a number of block quotations. We teach our students to avoid block quotations in their essays except when breaking up the language of the speaker would risk losing the continuity of the original argument or diminish the rhetorical or literary effect intended. The block quotations herein were written and spoken aloud by some of the greatest orators of the antebellum period. I suggest that rather than cut and feed all of them piecemeal into paraphrases, readers should try to speak them aloud, savoring the dramatic impact of the words and traveling back through them to the time and place in which they were delivered.

For comments I am grateful to Williamjames Hull Hoffer, coeditor of the series; my longtime collaborator N. E. H. Hull; my University of Georgia colleague Stephen Berry; Vernon Burton, a friend and expert on the period; and John David Smith, whose gracious reading for Johns Hopkins University Press and for me was the sine qua non for publication. Elizabeth Demers guided the book through the press. Without her confidence in the project, it would not have seen the light of day. Joanne Allen did a superb job of copyediting. To Brian Wheel, formerly my editor at Oxford University Press, who saw merit in the initial project, I wish the best of luck in all his future endeavors.

JOHN QUINCY ADAMS AND THE
GAG RULE, 1835–1850

"John Quincy Adams Goes to Congress"

IN DECEMBER 1835, former US president John Quincy Adams returned to his seat in the Massachusetts delegation to the House of Representatives. Stocky, at sixty-eight visibly ailing from years abroad as a diplomat
and a more recent troubled stint as chief executive, Adams was after a fashion
the last puritan in America. Deeply religious, suspicious of the motives of his
enemies (who were legion), passionately loyal to his friends, he suffered no
fools, gladly or otherwise. Though nominally a National Republican, after
that party had become the Whigs Adams abjured all party connections. He
hated slavery but was not an active abolitionist. He spoke often in Congress
on a wide variety of issues, but slavery was not often one of them.

That December, the nation's capital was frozen over, shivering through
some of the lowest temperatures in the city's history. The cold turned the
mud accumulating on the cobbled streets to gray-green stone. From his own
home, books, pamphlets, newspapers, and his own writings, primarily drafts
of speeches, spilling out from his study, Adams muffled himself in woolens
and walked to the Capitol. He was almost always the first to arrive in the
House of Representatives chamber, and his attendance record was legend-
ary. There he took a seat in the front row of the half circle of desks jammed

together facing the raised podium of the speaker. Seat assignment was first come, first seated, and because of his failing hearing, Adams wanted to be near the speakers. The front row also gave him an advantage when he sought to be recognized by the Speaker, James K. Polk, of Tennessee. During the session he rarely left his desk save to greet visiting constituents who wanted to shake the great man's hand. Like one of the many pillars in the chamber that kept its vaulted dome in place, Adams seemed a fixture of the House from his first term in 1830 until he died in 1848.

On this day, December 21, Congressmen read petitions sent them by constituents, a practice observed in the lower house before the formal session got under way. Sometimes the petitioner wanted Congress to pass a "special bill" to aid a person in need. The abolitionists had begun a letter-writing and petitioning campaign that summer, and now some of their petitions waited in the queue. Custom dictated that the reading of petitions begin with Maine and work its way south and west through the states. One of the Maine petitions called for the abolition of slavery in the District of Columbia, whose governance lay in the hands of the Congress.

As Representative James Fairfield dutifully read the petition, Adams listened with only one ear. President Andrew Jackson had sent a message to Congress regarding a bequest to the country from an Englishman, James Smithson, for the "founding of an establishment for the increase and diffusion of knowledge among men." An ad hoc committee had been formed, to which Adams had been named. When it came time for Massachusetts to present its petitions, however, Adams sat up and paid attention, for the inhabitants of Holliston had sent a petition "preying Congress to provide for the immediate abolition of slavery and the slave trade in the District of Columbia." It was moved, as was the custom, that the petition be referred to the Committee on the District. Newly elected South Carolina Democrat James Henry Hammond objected. He wanted Congress to "reject" the petition.

There was a precedent for this, though Hammond did not cite it, and the members, save those from Virginia, may not have been aware of it. After the Nat Turner rebellion in Southampton County, Virginia, in 1830, the legislature had taken up the matter of a petition for the gradual manumission of the state's slaves the next year. The authors were Quakers and the member who presented it was William Roane, scion of one of the state's leading families. Like John Quincy Adams, he was not an abolitionist, but he wanted the matter debated. William Goode objected. He wanted the petition trashed without debate. The House of Delegates voted 93 to 27 to debate the petition. In Congress, the members present voted on Hammond's motion, and to Adams's pleasure, 115 members agreed that the petitions should not be summarily rejected. But 100 members agreed with Hammond. And that was just the beginning.[1]

Chattel slavery, the treatment of men and women as personal property rather than persons, was disappearing from the Western world in the 1830s but remained entrenched in one portion of the United States. White southern leaders called it their "peculiar institution" and defended it as a public and private good. Not all of their countrymen agreed. Slaves resisted their bondage in a variety of ways, including running away. When they departed, they fled to the "free states" in the North or to Canada. Many white northerners were morally and spiritually opposed to chattel slavery and harbored or abetted the runaways. Such moral convictions had not yet turned into a major public campaign when the decade of the 1830s opened, however. Indeed, white public opinion in favor of the abolition of slavery was very slow in forming. The debates over the gag rule changed all this, moving the sectional quarrel over slavery in the South to the center of national politics.[2]

John Quincy Adams always abhorred slavery. He thought it a "curse" inconsistent with the liberties for which the Revolution had been fought and the republic established. But Adams was a lawyer, and he knew that slavery had been established by law in one-half of the nation. Indeed, without the sanction of law, slavery would have been the crime of man-stealing. He believed that the economic benefits of slavery to the owners of slaves had perverted their moral instincts. But facts were facts, and slavery was a fact that even the most decent and clever congressional debater apparently had to accept, or so it seemed.[3]

The public debate over slavery in the United States began at the Constitutional Convention in 1787 and thereafter erupted only periodically until the events traced in this volume. True, when the debate did erupt, it was highly divisive. At first, the abolition of all slaves by law had few advocates. The focus of the debate was ending the international slave trade. During the debates in 1819–21 over the admission of Missouri to statehood, the focus of the controversy shifted to the expansion of slavery into the territories. In addition, opponents of slavery were urging slave owners to voluntarily free their slaves (manumission). Not until the debate from 1835 to 1850 over the gag rule, to use the term Adams coined, did the focus become the end of slavery as a national institution. By the time Congress considered the Compromise of 1850, every speech on the admission of California as a free state, the Fugitive Slave Bill, and the abolition of slave sales in the District of Columbia included either an attack on or a defense of slavery.

The gag rule was a House procedural measure, a resolution to reject out of hand all antislavery petitions, passed at the beginning of each session from 1836 through 1840, when it was made a standing rule of the House, and finally rescinded at the end 1844. In the Senate, a similar rule lasted until 1850. As is so often the case in lawmaking, procedure and substance were intertwined. Strongly pressed by South Carolina's delegation in Congress, for a time supported by all southern and some northern Democratic congressmen, the gag rule became a proxy defense of slavery's morality and economic value.

At first only a few members of Congress objected to the gag rule. These antislavery representatives argued strongly for the reception and reading of the petitions. When they found an almost uniformly hostile audience, Adams, a former secretary of state and president of the United States then representing a constituency in Plymouth, Massachusetts, opened a second front. He saw the effort to gag the petitioners as a violation of their constitutional rights. His campaign to lift the gag rule, joined each year by more and more northern members of Congress, revealed how the slavery issue promoted a virulent sectionalism and ultimately played a part in southern secession and the Civil War.

Returning to examine the gag-rule debates in Congress allows us to revisit a time when oratory and rhetoric mattered to American politicians. Unlike our own times of spin and campaign donations from giant political-action committees, it was a time when politicians wrote the words they spoke and when their words actually affected the course of politics. Throughout its course, the gag-rule battle featured dramatic oratory. How could it be otherwise, when the cast of characters included not only Adams but also forceful abolitionists like William Slade of Vermont and Joshua Giddings of Ohio and fierce defenders of the South's "peculiar institution" of slavery like Senator John C. Calhoun and Representatives James Henry Hammond and Henry F. Wise?

There is both repetitiveness and change in the oratory reported in the *Register of Debates* and the *Congressional Globe*. Certain themes were present throughout the entirety of the debates: disputes over the meaning of the

Constitution, the character of the petitioners, and the morality of slavery. The debates also had a kind of internal logic, that is, a process by which new issues arose out of old ones. The new issues might be entirely unexpected, even unwanted, by members. For example, at first the debates did not set North against South—merely anti- against proslavery thought. But as the debates wore on, the language shifted to a sectional one, a kind of shorthand in which North and South replaced anti- and proslavery stances. This shift in turn promoted an increasingly divisive sectionalism, with nuance and moderation giving way to stiff-necked accusations and counteraccusations.

The official record of the debate also features a kind of subtext. One has to read between the lines of the speeches to gain their full meaning. Members of Congress were familiar with one another's arguments, but the modern newcomer to the debates has to follow them from their inception to discover what past events or ideas speakers referenced. The debates were an extended conversation over a long period of time among men who did not have to explain themselves to one another.

Of course, members were not only speaking to one another on these occasions; they were speaking for and to their respective constituencies. Members of the House faced elections every two years, and while most of the members were routinely returned to their seats, reapportionment, political realignments, and personal issues led to departures and arrivals. Adams was there for the entire period, but Hammond left at the end of the Twenty-First Congress and did not return to Congress until the 1850s. Most often, the members said what they wanted voters to hear, and this in turn reflected what they expected voters to favor. Most of these members, however, did not regard themselves as mere delegates, mouthpieces for their constituents. Instead, they saw themselves as trustees for their constituents' interests. They might thus lag behind or run ahead of public opinion. On top of this, certain members took others' comments personally as assaults on their honor. Adams never fought a duel (he preferred to wage war with words), but others who played a major role in the debates, for example, Henry A. Wise, of Virginia, did. The real violence the vehemence of the debates portended, however, was just over the horizon. At least one "fire-eater" in the South, Robert Barnwell Rhett, attributed the coming conflict over secession to "the expedient of John Quincy Adams for emancipating our slaves," leading the way to the North's "dominion over us."[4]

1

"Slavery Cannot Be Abolished"

IN 1776, WHEN VIRGINIA'S THOMAS JEFFERSON told the world that "all men are created equal," slavery was everywhere in America. A few of the founding fathers, notably Aaron Burr, Alexander Hamilton, John Jay, Gouverneur Morris, and Rufus King, all from New York or Massachusetts, had wanted the end of slavery, but these men were hardly abolitionists. They were emancipationists who wanted slave owners to manumit, or free, their slaves voluntarily. Jay, shortly to become the first chief justice of the US Supreme Court, nevertheless confided to an English antislavery advocate in 1788, "It is not easy to persuade men in general to act on that magnanimous and disinterested principle. It is well known that errors, either in opinion or practice, long entertained or indulged, are difficult to eradicate, and particularly so when they have become, as it were, incorporated in the civil institutions and domestic economy of a whole people."[1]

None of the Virginians among the founders, including Jefferson, James Madison, and George Washington, went as far in condemnation of slavery as Jay and his fellow northerners. They thought slavery an evil, to be sure. As Jefferson wrote in his *Notes on the State of Virginia* (1781–85), slavery had "an unhappy influence on the manners of our people." The people were the free white population, whose passions were aroused by the "despotism" of masters and the "degrading submission" of the slaves. It was an evil combination for which there was no easy solution, however, save the voluntary decision of masters not to augment the number of slaves in the state. Jefferson did not include in this calculation the natural increase of slave numbers through birth (a process in which he was to participate later in his life). Madison owned about one hundred slaves at his death and did not free any of them in his will. He did think that "a general emancipation of slaves ought to be 1. gradual. 2. equitable & satisfactory to the individuals immediately concerned. 3. consistent with the existing & durable prejudices of the nation." But when one of his slaves, Billy, ran away and was recaptured, Madison freed him "for coveting the liberty for which we have paid the price of so much blood, and have proclaimed so often to be the right, and worthy the pursuit, of every human being." Washington arranged to free his slaves after the demise of his wife Martha, but he bought and sold slaves, and when they disobeyed him, he arranged for their sale to less healthy climes than his Virginia estates. The maintenance of a union of slave and free states was more important than any general plan of emancipation, and that meant that rancorous debate over slavery's fate must be "put to rest."[2]

Despite the entreaties of Washington and others to lay aside disputes over slavery, Quaker proponents of the early end of the overseas slave trade petitioned Congress to promote their cause. The first debate in Congress over these petitions, from February to March 1790, fulfilled Jay's prediction that the mere mention of manumission would arouse passion. Members debated what to do with the petitions and in the course of the debate confronted the question whether the new Constitution gave the federal government the power to do anything about slavery. Or did the constitutional compromises on slavery, such as the Three-Fifths Clause, include, imply, or require a ban on the discussion of slavery?[3]

William Loughton Smith, of South Carolina, explained why his state thought the petitions should not be debated at all. "Mr. Smith said he lamented much that this subject had been brought before the House . . . because he foresaw that it would produce a very unpleasant discussion." This was how a self-styled gentleman protested. Had he protested with more vehemence, or with more passionate language, he might have found himself challenged to a duel. (One such duel, between Congressman Matthew Lyon of Vermont and Roger Griswold of Connecticut in 1798, would become a cause

Washington as a Farmer at Mount Vernon, by Junius Brutus Stearns, 1858. This idyllic view of Washington's slave force at Mount Vernon shows children playing as Washington instructs an overseer. He had hundreds of slaves, and while he was a relatively humane master, he would not tolerate misconduct. Courtesy of Library of Congress.

célèbre in the House.) Smith warned that "this was a subject of a nature to excite the alarms of the southern members, who could not view, without anxiety, any interference in it on the part of Congress." Southern representatives feared that such petitions, in the wrong hands, could provoke slave insurrections. Although such insurrections were few and far between, members all knew about the Stono River, South Carolina, slave rebellion of 1739, in which dozens of whites and hundreds of blacks had died, and the prospect of such an event recurring in South Carolina was truly horrific. In addition, "the memorials from the Quakers contained, in his opinion, a very indecent attack on the character of those states which possess slaves. It [the petitions] reprobates slavery as bringing down reproach on the southern states, and expiated on the detestation due to the licentious wickedness of the African [slave] trade and the inhuman tyranny and blood guiltiness inseparable from it." Personal honor was much prized among the planter classes, but personal honor was not the only reason to object to the material in the petitions. "He then showed that all the state governments clearly retained all the rights of sovereignty which they had before the establishment of the Constitution, unless they were exclusively delegated to the United States; and this could only exist where the Constitution granted, in express terms, an exclusive authority to the Union." This states'-rights constitutional argument was one that would run through the slavery debates in Congress like a red thread.[4]

Smith regarded the language of the petitions as a slur on the morality of his fellow white southerners. He rejected the Quakers' condemnations of slavery as "indecent" insofar as they held white southerners up as "men divested of every principle of honor and humanity." He then read portions of Jefferson's *Notes on the State of Virginia* that said in effect that every white person, even those who wanted the slave trade to end, found association with people of color abhorrent. He devoted the rest of his two-hour-long speech to offering illustrations of the universality of slavery.[5]

The opponents of receiving the petitions did not, however, wish to muzzle the petitioners or their representatives in Congress. They simply wanted the petitions to lie lifeless on the Speaker's desk, dead letters. Were such petitions given serious consideration, the result would be, in the words of one southern member, "a civil war." The situation in the House, noted the visiting senator William Maclay of Pennsylvania, was growing "tense." Members from Upper South states like Maryland called for calm and reassured their Deep South colleagues that the only reason to placate the petitioners was their right to petition for redress of grievances. General emancipation was not the issue; even the petitioners were not calling for it. House members finally compromised by automatically referring the petitions to committee, without debate.[6]

In 1790, members of Congress may have assumed that slavery would die of its own accord. Jefferson confidently told the visiting French aristocrat the duc de la Rochefoucauld that slavery and slaves would soon vanish from the new republic. The introduction of widespread cotton cultivation in the late 1790s, along with the expansion of the United States into the western territories, reinvigorated the institution of slavery, however. Slave labor in the cotton fields, along with rice and sugar cultivation, made slavery even more profitable than it had been in the first decade of the new nation. Not only was the labor of the bondmen and bondwomen a boon to large-scale production but the internal slave trade and the natural (birth) increase of slaves added to the institution's profitability. The shipment of raw southern cotton to northern textile mills meant profits for both regions. Still, one can ask whether the slavery issue in Congress quieted as a result of silent compromise between sections or was unripe for serious reconsideration. In fact, northern states proceeded to end slavery slowly and irregularly. Upper South states made manumission easier, and some Lower South spokesmen opined that slavery would gradually disappear. Perhaps a national conversation on the future of slavery was unnecessary.[7]

As slavery expanded to the newly opened territory of the Southwest, however, so did the potential for contention about slavery. Although antislavery agitation was not a major or ongoing preoccupation of American politicians, whenever the slavery issue did arise in national politics, as in the debate over the admission of Missouri as a slave state from 1819 through 1821, it paralyzed Congress and resulted in sharp divisions, overheated rhetoric, and threats of dismemberment of the Union. When Missouri applied for statehood with a constitution legalizing slavery, tempers in Congress once again flared. "Yield nothing" was for a time the watchword of both sides in the lower house. In time, cooler heads prevailed in the Senate. As a result, the leaders of the major political parties agreed to a series of compromises designed less to resolve differences over slavery than to disguise the extent and consequences of those differences. Nevertheless, the Missouri Compromise left the nation holding "a wolf by the ear."[8]

The on-again, off-again consensus in the House to avoid the slavery issue collapsed when abolitionist agitation moved into a new, more strident phase. Earlier antislavery efforts had entailed the purchase and relocation of slaves to an African home by the American Colonization Society. The colonization plan was entirely voluntary, as was the gradual emancipation movement, intended to persuade slave owners to free their slaves. Neither of these movements made much headway after 1815 in the Deep South, where slave labor was a vital part of staple crop agriculture and the sale of surplus slave labor was a major source of income. In states like South Carolina, even the whisper of emancipation led to public rebuke and the threat of violence.[9]

Proslavery violence had the unintended effect of angering and emboldening the opponents of slavery. Led by publicists like William Lloyd Garrison, editor of the antislavery newspaper the *Liberator*, and ministers like Theodore Dwight Weld, a group of committed antislavery men and women formed the

American Anti-Slavery Society in 1833 and demanded the immediate end to slavery. While they did not wield political power—they held no public offices—these abolitionists were "supreme organizers and agitators." Though few in number, they were aided by innovations in technology, in particular the technology of the presses. Whether prompted by fierce moralism, romantic idealism, or simply repulsion at slavery, they pressed their demands on the public. Even before he spearheaded the creation of the American Anti-Slavery Society, Garrison collected and republished antislavery materials along with his own editorial views in the *Liberator*. The very first issue set this tone.

> For the successful prosecution of our labors, we appeal to the following classes of our fellow countrymen, and we presume they are sufficiently numerous to fulfil our expectations:
>
> *To the religious*—who profess to walk in the footsteps of their Divine Master, and to be actuated by a love which worketh no ill to others. To whom, if not to them, shall we turn for encouragement?
>
> *To the philanthropic*—who show their sincerity by their works, whose good deeds are more numerous than their professions, who not only pity but relieve.
>
> *To the patriotic*—who love their country better than themselves, and would avert its impending ruin.
>
> *To the ignorant, the cold-hearted, the base*, the tyrannical—who need to be instructed, and quickened, and reclaimed, and humanized.[10]

Garrison's convictions were the product of firsthand experience with slavery in Baltimore. Weld's commitment came from a deeply religious source. Along with Weld, a coterie of ministers and seminary students joined the movement. In the same years that Garrison was publishing antislavery pamphlets in the *Liberator*, Weld and his coworkers set about collecting firsthand accounts of the conditions of slavery from a wide variety of sources, including emancipated and runaway slaves. In 1839 they published *American Slavery As It Is*. Their purpose was to refute the argument of defenders of slavery who depicted slavery as a gentle and uplifting way of life. The very first passages in the book summarized their argument and indirectly illustrated why defenders of slavery had for the past decade regarded the abolitionist movement as dangerously incendiary.[11]

The masthead of the *Liberator* changed over time, but the images were always striking depictions of the degradation of slavery, such as whippings, and the virtue of emancipation. Courtesy of Library of Congress.

The language was certainly not what Smith had used, for the abolitionists did not regard themselves as gentlemen. They were reformers, and reformers in this romantic age were permitted to appeal to the heart as well as the head. The way to rouse the spirit of free persons from their slumbers was to pour on the rhetorical effects. "We repeat it, every man knows that slavery is a curse. Whoever denies this, his lips libel his heart. Try him; clank the chains in his ears, and tell him they are for *him*; give him an hour to prepare his wife and children for a life of slavery; bid him make haste and get necks for the yoke, and their wrists for the coffle chains, then look at his pale lips and trembling knees, and you have *nature's* testimony against slavery." The enormity of the sin was multiplied by the size of the institution. "Two millions seven hundred thousand persons in these States are in this condition. They were made slaves and are held such by force, and by being put in fear, and this for no crime! Reader, what have you to say of such treatment?" Weld and his coworkers did not propose to wait for an answer. "Suppose I should seize you, rob you of your liberty, drive you into the field, and make you work without pay as long as you live, would that be justice and kindness, or monstrous injustice and cruelty? Now, every body knows that the slaveholders do these things to the slaves every day, and yet it is stoutly affirmed that they treat them well and kindly, and that their tender regard for their slaves restrains the masters from inflicting cruelties upon them."[12]

The *Liberator* did not have a wide circulation, and *American Slavery as It Is* was hardly a bestseller, but another of the tools the advocates of immediate emancipation adopted did reach a wider, more influential audience. The abolitionists used the mails. They flooded the nation's post offices with abolitionist literature. The idea was not his in origin, but it struck Garrison "like a thunderbolt." The petitions were part of this postal campaign. They could swell the number of abolitionists not just as a way of energizing a latent reformism; the thousands of petitioners were a kind of proxy electorate, because the petitions were sent to Congress.[13]

The right to petition the government for redress of grievance was guaranteed to Americans in the First Amendment. In 1835, the First Amendment only applied to the federal government, but various states had included the right to petition in their constitutions. South Carolina's constitution was an exception. But even southern opponents of the petitioning conceded that point. In theory, petitioning was one way in which those who had no direct communication with those in power could inform the government of injustice or simply complain. As such, it might have been described as the right to make a fuss. But the historical purpose of such petitions was a redress of grievances. These might be private or public. A private grievance could be resolved by a private bill, a kind of legislative relief. A public grievance was a different matter and required a review of policy and law generally. The right to petition did not mean that the petitions would be heeded or even read. Insofar as the federal Constitution, the Fugitive Slave Act of 1793, various slave-state constitutions, and a series of cases in which the US Supreme Court provided support for federal and state laws upholding slavery, the antislavery petitions required a thorough—and thoroughly unlikely—revision of federal law.[14]

Still, what hope did this band of abolitionists have of influencing anyone? The answer lay in their effort itself: to force the North to face its complicity, or at least its compliance, in the existence of slavery in the South. The most common target of these petitions was the slave trade in the nation's capital, the city of Washington in the District of Columbia. The district was administered by Congress. The theoretical question was whether that authority would allow Congress to end slavery in the district. A less comprehensive question was whether Congress could suppress the slave trade in the District. As Congress had already legislated against the international slave trade, the latter question was capable of a solution, and in fact in 1850 Congress did ban slave auctions in the District.

But in 1835 Washington DC was a largely southern city in which slavery and the slave trade were legal, the slave auctions in public reminded politicians from the free states how potent the slave lobby was, and the petitions underscored the point. Many of these petitions, like letters to members of Congress today, were "boilerplate"; that is, they were preprinted, so that the petitioners just had to fill in the blanks. They looked like the one reproduced below, preserved in the Moore Family Papers at Old Sturbridge Village, Massachusetts. It was dated 1835 and came from "the Ladies."

TO THE CONGRESS OF THE UNITED STATES

YOUR PETITIONERS, Ladies of the town of _____, in the county of _____, and state of _____, beg leave to represent to your honorable body, that the people of the United States have vested in Congress, by the first Article of the Federal Constitution, "exclusive legislation, in all cases whatsoever," over the District of Columbia.

Your Petitioners do not ask your honorable body to legislate for the abolition of slavery in the several states where it exists, but they do respectfully represent that duty to their country, to mankind, and to God, forbids Congress to exercise their power of "exclusive legislation," to PERPETUATE SLAVERY AND THE SLAVE TRADE in the Capital of the American Republic. The acts of Congress hitherto passed for the government of said District in fact do this.

If these laws are ever to be repealed, and slavery and the slave trade in that District are thereby ever to cease, it must be by the action of Congress. Your Petitioners believe that no time can be more favorable for such action than the present. They therefore most respectfully but earnestly entreat your honorable body to pass without delay such laws, as to your wisdom may seem right and proper for the entire abolition of slavery and the slave trade in the District of Colombia.

The thousands of petitions sent to Congress were part of a lobbying attempt far out of proportion to the political power behind them. Most white northerners were either indifferent to the plight of the slaves or actively opposed the idea of emancipation. That did not deter a mob from routinely breaking into the post office in Charleston and seizing and destroying abolitionist literature. In response to this violation of federal law (it was a felony to steal the post), President Andrew Jackson, a slaveholder himself, called for a ban on the mailing of abolitionist literature.[15]

The petitions asked Congress to end slavery in the District of Columbia. Their reception was debated on the floor of both houses. The long reign of the resulting gag rules and the surrounding controversy marked the end of the phony peace over slavery and foretold the coming conflict.

As the December 1835 session of the Twenty-Fourth Congress opened, the slavery issue, which had long lurked in the corridors of the Capitol, entered its legislative chambers. The first business of the day was the reading of petitions, and James Fairfield, representing York County, Maine, rose to present a petition from the 172 ladies of the county begging Congress to end slavery in the District. Two days later, on December 18, 1835, James Henry Hammond, of South Carolina, responded with a novel proposal. Previously, the petitions had been summarily laid on the table or referred to the Committee on the District of Columbia, where they would die a slow death. Hammond wanted the House to reject them outright. They were, he believed, an insult to the honor of the South.

Hammond married into great wealth, eventually owning more than three hundred slaves. In the course of his career he was a newspaper publisher, a schoolteacher, a lawyer, and a politician whose support for slavery, nullification, and, later, secession never wavered. A first-term congressman in the Twenty-Fourth Congress, he left the body after that term. Later he was elected governor of South Carolina, and then he returned to Congress as a senator in the last session before the Civil War. For a time, unwonted dalliances (today we would call them sexual abuses) with his teenaged nieces cost him his reputation, but his fierce support for the South's peculiar institution eventually restored him to good public graces in South Carolina. In December 1835, he told the other members of the South Carolina delegation who roomed with him in Washington that for him the rejection of the petitions was a matter of the deepest and most important principles.[16]

Hammond's comments were not just procedural. He and those who later supported his resolution called the abolitionists bloodthirsty creatures who would set the slaves on their masters. No southern woman or child (he did not say, but he meant white woman or child) would be safe from the innately savage Africans if they were freed from their bondage (or if they had access to abolitionist writings). Hammond judged that it was necessary to "put a more decided seal of reprobation" on the petitions. Hammond's proposal was

"THE HOME OF THE OPPRESSED."

CAPITOL OF THE UNITED STATES.   "HAIL COLUMBIA."

Slavery was alive and well in the District of Columbia until the Civil War, though the number of free persons of color was more than three times the number of slaves. The auction of slaves was forbidden by Congress in the Compromise of 1850, and in 1862 Congress provided for compensated manumission. Print published by the American Anti-Slavery Society, 1836. Courtesy of Library of Congress.

seconded by Virginia's John Mercer Patton, who said that he wished to "quiet" the anxiety raised by the reading of the petitions. Patton's was a less confrontational strand in the argument for the gag rule. That anxiety was shared by his fellow southern members and presumably the white citizens of his district.[17]

On December 23, Congressman William Slade of Vermont raised the stakes. Slade not only read another petition but urged (as Fairfield had not) that the prayers of his petitioner ladies be answered by Congress. In the course of his remarks, he mentioned the "evils of slavery" and said that the petition was one Congress must consider. Two days later, after the attempted reading of another petition, Hammond moved that it and all such petitions not be received at all.[18]

As Hammond's request was unprecedented, a number of members objected to it, and Hammond himself modified it to reject the petition at hand. Again, as in 1790, members from the border states tried to end any controversy by simply continuing the automatic tabling of the petitions. Hammond's pressure to reject the DC slavery petitions, however, had the support of other Deep South members, and without meaning to, their plan brought the issue of slavery itself to the floor. Henceforth, no one would confine himself to the question of procedure. Representative Francis Thomas, a Jacksonian Democrat from Maryland, summarized what he saw as the shifting focus of the debate: "He was surprised to discover that there were gentlemen who were not content with the evidence which has already been given, that a very large majority of this house are opposed to any interference whatever not only with the rights of slaveholders in the southern states, but with the existence of slavery within the District of Columbia." There followed not a short exposition of the prior motions but the first of many long speeches on slavery.[19]

The genie was now out of the bottle, and no one could, or seemed to want to, put it back. A series of votes to avoid the issue of slavery only led to more speeches on it. Adams had voted with the majority to refer the petition to the Committee on the District. At least the petition would be officially received rather than rejected. The brief effort at conciliation seemed to continue as Waddy Thompson, of South Carolina, assured the members of the House that he was not about to look for sinister and bad motives on the part of the petitioners themselves nor those members who presented the petitions. To do so would be to cross a line of civility in the lower house that no one, not even Hammond, had yet crossed.

But Slade was getting what he wanted: a debate. As much as members from the South protested that Congress had no power to touch slavery where it existed, their protestations revealed their anxiety that the federal government, moved by the petitions or other efforts of the abolitionists, might regulate slavery. The members demanded, in the words of Representative Henry Wise of Virginia, that "Congress expressly disclaim any such power, in order that the people of the North may understand it will be in vain for them to offer such petitions"; to that end, they wished to reconsider the vote referring the petition, without debate, to the committee. Wise agreed with Hammond that they should reject the petitions outright.[20]

Slade's substantial contribution to that debate came five days later, on December 23. "He approached the subject . . . with an oppressive sense of its magnitude, and knowing its exciting character, of the great danger of being betrayed, in the progress of its discussion, into a state of feeling, unsuited to the place and the occasion. . . . He begged gentlemen [i.e., other members] to

James Henry Hammond, of Columbia, South Carolina, early in his career found the life of the plantation gentleman much to his liking.

believe . . . that he should say nothing intended to give the slightest personal offense to any."[21]

Slade began with something like Thomas's and Thompson's moderation. In this period, Congress was still the home of polite oratory. While "stump" speakers rousing crowds of voters on election day might assail their opponents with inflammatory language, members of Congress were expected to avoid personal attacks. The standing rules of the House forbade such conduct. So Slade began with an almost studied caution. But even as he denied any descent into name-calling, he admitted that he would address the "magnitude" of the issue; that is, he was going to talk about not only the petitions but also slavery and freedom. "These petitioners, as far as he was acquainted with them, were among the most intelligent and respectable of the community in which they reside, while the subject of their petitions was one of which it well became them to speak."[22]

Slade may or may not have known all the petitioners—after all, there was

William Slade of Vermont in the 1840s. Slade was a major player in Vermont politics but not in national politics and not in Congress. A reformer of the conservative type, he crusaded for compulsory public education after his retirement from politics. Original in Vermont Historical Society, Montpelier.

a boilerplate character to the lists of signers as well as to the text of the petitions—but he knew that the movement did not enroll street people. These were men and women of property and standing, the bedrock of northern respectability. The very idea of democracy rested upon the participation of such people in the public affairs of the nation. They were also his constituents, just as slaveholders were among the constituents of the southern members. Slade was a lawyer, an editor, and a reporter of the decisions of the Vermont Supreme Court before he was elected to Congress, and after he served, he was elected governor of Vermont. In short, he was a man of serious legal and personal demeanor, not a rabble-rouser at all.

> I am in favor of the prayer of the petitioners. I believe that Congress has a right to legislate on the subject, and that the time has come when it ought to legislate. . . . Let me not be misunderstood. The abolition of slavery which I would advocate is a gradual abolition. I believe the immediate and unqualified abolition of slavery to be inconsistent with a just regard, both to the best interests of the community and the highest welfare of the slave. . . . I would not render worse the condition of the slave, by conferring upon him rights which he is not fitted to enjoy, and which would become to him a curse rather than a blessing. I would not, at once, entirely emancipate him from the control of his master. . . . I would not confer upon him the same rights which are possessed by his master, and for the obvious reason that he is not fitted to enjoy them. . . . We owe it to this degraded race of men to prepare them for freedom, to communicate to

them moral and religious and literary instruction, to restore and protect the domestic relations among them.

Slade assumed that the arguments defenders of slavery made were true, that slaves were not ready for freedom and that they were not the equals of their masters. He thus reified the master and the slave, assuming that all masters were alike and all slaves were alike. That meant that no slave was capable of freedom and no slave was the equal of any white person. He did not credit the fact that some free persons of color and some runaway or freed slaves were already the equals of more than one free person. With the exception of a handful of abolitionists, the North willingly surrendered to the pernicious influence of racism and the odious overgeneralization among northern intellectuals that passed for science.[23]

Slade's moderation was studied, meant to conciliate rather than inflame his southern colleagues. "I admire indeed the purity of the philanthropy which seeks to abolish the institution of slavery, and elevate the degraded children of Africa from the condition of poverty to the privileges of men, but I deplore its often misdirected zeal, and deprecate the reaction which it is calculated to produce." His abolitionism was of the gradualist type: "The abolition of slavery in the [slave] states must be their own work. To convince them that the whole system is ruinous and wrong, is not the labor of a day or a year." Slade's gradualist position was at odds with the abolitionist postal campaign, and he surely knew it, but he assumed that "the sentiments of the people of the north" were more in accord with his. In fact, antiabolitionist riots were breaking out all over the North, even in Garrison's hometown of Boston. People of standing and influence led mobs who did not want to compete with cheap African American labor. Nor did these same northern mobs want the social and domestic mixing of the races.[24]

Slade was also aware of the British experiment with halfway emancipation in the sugar-island colonies, so-called apprenticeship. In 1833, Parliament provided for the gradual emancipation of adult slaves to begin in 1834 and last until 1838. They were to be indentured servants to their masters. The experiment failed, however, as indentured servitude poorly served both former slaves and former masters. Full freedom came in 1836.[25]

The opening of each session of Congress brought new petitions. Responding to another spate of antislavery petitions at the next meeting of Congress, on February 1, 1836, Hammond again called for a blanket rejection of all antislavery petitions. Hammond made clear his objections to the petitions but went beyond procedural questions to refute Slade's condemnation of slavery. He avowed his "sacred regard for the inestimable right of petition" but said that Congress's refusal to receive such petitions did not deny anyone's right to petition. It was a clever move and might have closed the debate with a whimper, but Hammond could not restrain himself. Inadvertently, Hammond was to do just what the petitioners wanted Slade to do: make slavery itself the focus of the debate. For Hammond saw abolitionism as a kind of contagion that must be quarantined. "From this moment [the 1833 convention of the American Anti-Slavery Society] the infection spread with unparalleled rapidity."[26]

Hammond read from the society's literature, saying, for example, "here sir is the prospectus of the sixth volume of the Liberator," to the effect that he was exposing the abolitionists' "party warfare." Actually he was giving their views more publicity than Slade had. Did Hammond realize that rehearsing at such length the views of the abolitionists did exactly what they wanted? At the very least, Hammond was guilty of accusing all abolitionists of planning what the most verbally extreme of them warned, that is, slave rebellion. In true Ciceronian fashion he said exactly what he promised not to say: "I will not inflict a review of this work on the House. . . . I ask pardon of the House for using such emphatic language . . . but when a . . . more detested monster [threatens] to steep our land in blood, and cover it with ashes, it becomes everyone to expose, in plain language, the honest indignation of his heart."[27]

The contagion posed the greatest danger to his own homeland, not the nation but the slaveholding regions. "There can no longer be a doubt of the deep, pervading, uncontrollable excitement which shakes the free states on this subject, nor of the energy and power with which the abolitionists are pressing their made and fatal schemes." Was this an example of paranoia? The abolitionists certainly wanted their influence to appear all-powerful, but as other members of the House had correctly informed Hammond, the abolitionist movement was small and politically unimportant. It was hard to tell on what evidence, other than the abolitionist publications he had gathered, Hammond's fears were based. Had he traveled the North, gaining firsthand information, those fears might have been allayed. There were southerners who did travel in the North, and they were not pleased by what they saw and heard, but they did not find a groundswell of proabolitionist sentiment.[28]

Hammond wanted it understood that southern manhood, a pervasive subtheme of his oration, was not threatened by the fear of a slave uprising but concerned about its likelihood. "There may be nervous men and timid women, whose imaginations are haunted with unwonted fears, among us . . . but in no part of the world have men of ordinary firmness less fear of danger from their operatives than we have. . . . During the two hundred years that slavery has existed in their country there has, I believe, been one serious insurrection, and that one very limited in its extent." Hammond was referring to the Nat Turner rebellion in the counties south of Virginia's James River. That uprising, in 1830, had taken the lives of dozens of whites and three times the number of suspected rebels. But there had been an even more serious uprising on the German coast of Louisiana in 1811, involving hundreds of slaves; another (the Denmark Vesey affair) feared in Charleston in 1820, resulting in the execution of dozens of slaves; and still another (Gabriel's Rebellion) planned in Richmond in 1800. Major slave rebellions on the Caribbean islands were well reported in the South, and white refugees from the Haitian rebellion of 1795 flooded into Charleston. The state's system of nighttime patrols and freeholders' courts (no juries for slave suspects) was an effective means of controlling large-scale rebellions, but many small rebellions took the form of running away, breaking tools, work slowdowns, and other forms of daily resistance by slaves to slavery. Slaveholders well knew the dangers to themselves and to their families of holding men and women in bondage.[29]

The abolitionist claim was at heart a moral one and had to be resisted forthrightly. "Slavery is said to be an evil . . . but it is no evil," stated Hammond. "On the contrary, I believe it to be the greatest of all great blessings that Providence has bestowed upon our glorious region." Hammond, a relatively new slave owner and planter, rested morality on economic progress. "For without [slavery], our fertile soil and our fructifying climate would have been given to us in vain." This assertion might or might not be true—some modern scholarship supports it—but Hammond could not rest his defense of slavery on purely entrepreneurial grounds. "And as to its impoverishing and demoralizing influence, the simple and irresistible answer to that is, that the history of the short period during which we have enjoyed it has rendered our southern country proverbial for its wealth, its genius, and its manners." In short, "Slavery cannot be abolished."[30]

Of course, theoretically, since slavery rested on positive law, changing the law to make slavery illegal would effactually abolish it. What Hammond meant was that abolition was political suicide for the nation. "The moment this House undertakes to legislate upon this subject, it dissolves the Union. Should it be my fortune to have a seat upon this floor, I will abandon it the instant the first decisive step is taken, looking towards legislation on this subject. I will go home to preach, and if I can, to practice, disunion, and civil war." In fact, that is exactly what he did in 1860. He foresaw that "a revolution must ensure, and this republic sink in blood. . . . These opinions, so natural, so strong, and so distinctly marking the geographical divisions of our country indicate difference which, if pushed much further, will inevitably separate us into two nations. A separation which I should regard as a calamity to the whole human race." This was the age of romantic oratory, with its heroic as well as its tragic inflections. Hammond's speech ended with a kind of elegy worth quoting in full. It captured elements of what would be called "manifest destiny," although the destiny in this case was a southern nation rather than the spread of American republicanism across the continent. Although the term came into common use in the 1840s, earlier versions of the notion were present in Benjamin Franklin's time. Note that *we* and *our* only referred to free persons. Slaves, after all, were property, not persons, belonging to their masters, not to themselves.[31]

Hammond's cast of mind was somewhat gloomy in the best of times. Facing the likelihood that abolitionism would not go away, he did not even allow himself to relish the prospect of victory. "Even if this House should refuse to receive these petitions, I am not one of those who permits himself to trust that the conflict will be at an end. Nor, sir, we shall still have to meet it elsewhere. We will meet it. It is our inevitable destiny to meet it in whatever shape it comes, or to whatever extremity it may go." If he was right, however, then the ultimate resolution of the petitions question was not an embargo on them or even the end of the petition campaign; it was the end of the union of free and slave states. "We may have to adopt an entire non-intercourse with the free states, and finally, sir, we may have to dissolve this Union. From none of these measures can we shrink, as circumstances may make them necessary."[32]

Convoyed by a flotilla of similar speeches, the South Carolina initiative to reject the petitions sailed ahead. Various plans for silencing the petitioners were referred to a special committee headed by South Carolina's Henry L. Pinckney, underlining the special interest that South Carolina had in the outcome. The committee and then the House struggled over how to phrase the committee resolution. Would it reject, refer, or table the petitions? Would it include a condemnation of the petitioners? At first, the resolution ended with a sop to the North, an afterthought that the petitioners need not be evil men and women. Even this palliative was unacceptable to Hammond and his allies. It was removed from the final version of the Pinckney committee's resolution of May 1836. The result was a vote on May 26 not to receive any of the petitions. The measure carried by a three-fifths majority, some of the free states' representatives wishing to maintain a studied silence on the slavery issue: "Resolved, That all petitions, memorials, resolutions, propositions, or papers, relating in any way or to any extent whatever to the subject of slavery, or the abolition of slavery, shall, without being either printed or referred, be laid upon the table, and that no further action whatever shall be had thereon."[33]

The resolution was bigger than the problem. On its way through the committee and then the whole House, the resolution grew to apply to all petitions, not just those aimed at slaves in the District of Columbia, and to all plans for a more general abolition. In other words, the resolution was a response to Slade's speech rather than to the petitions. As such, it would have gagged not only those members who wanted to introduce antislavery petitions but also those members who wanted to talk about the dangers or the end of slavery in a more general way. This is an example of how the logic of the argument altered the thinking of the members, causing them to adopt positions they had not fully explored at the outset of the debates. The *Richmond Enquirer* thus called the resolution part of its "anti-abolition" report, even though the resolution's original purpose was merely to prevent debate on the petitions.[34]

Meanwhile, in the Senate, Daniel Webster and other members were submitting antislavery petitions. In response, South Carolina's John C. Calhoun defended slavery as a reality that no oratory could change. Calhoun was the senior member of the South Carolina congressional delegation, and it is unlikely that Hammond acted without Calhoun's consent. Calhoun had served in both houses of Congress and as Andrew Jackson's vice president. He had been a nationalist in the 1810s and early 1820s but had become the constitutional advocate of states' rights when South Carolina protested against the Tariff of 1828. The secret author of its protest, in it Calhoun developed the idea of the concurrent majority, a "mutual negative among [the nation's] disparate interests." Although he fully elaborated on the doctrine by name in his *Disquisition on Government* in 1848, shortly before his death in 1850, the core idea was present in 1828. It justified a state's authority to "nullify" an act of

Congress that violated the state's rights (according to Calhoun's interpretation of the Constitution).[35]

On February 4, 1836, Calhoun reported the Senate's response to President Jackson's condemnation of the petitions and request for a law punishing anyone who prepared and sent such a petition to Congress. Far more than a response to the president, the report was an exploration of the entire question of antislavery and union. Calhoun, who had already secretly authored the foremost statement of states' rights in 1828, opened with a précis of that (nullification) doctrine: "The right of a state to defend itself against internal dangers is part of the great, primary, and inherent right of self defense, which, by the laws of nature, belongs to all communities." One might have regarded the nation as such a community and continued that slavery in one part of it subjected the whole to an internal danger, but Calhoun did not countenance this reading of the nullification doctrine. Instead, he only applied it to the southern section of the country. "having now shown that it [the right of self-defense against the abolitionists] belongs to the slaveholding states, whose institutions are in danger, and not to Congress," the relevant jurisdiction was that of the states, "within whose limits and jurisdiction the internal peace and security of the slaveholding states are endangered."[36]

One should note that Calhoun based the refusal to pass a federal law criminalizing the petitions on the very same states'-rights basis as his justification for nullification. He knew that South Carolina and other southern states were already entering post offices to seize and destroy abolitionist literature, which was a felony under existing federal law, though one that federal marshals were not pursuing in the South. Up to this point, Calhoun's argument was a dry constitutional exegesis, as one might expect from a lawyer of his high caliber. But he was not done, for he also posed as an economic and sociological expert on slavery.[37]

Calhoun's sociology of the South was hardly original, but it was not yet orthodoxy. There were still a few in the South, including planters' wives, who would not have agreed with it. Thus, like Hammond's view, it must be regarded as a masculine one. The master was a man, not a woman, and women's views had little place in it. "It must be born in mind that slavery as it exists in the Southern States . . . involves not only the master and slave, but, also, the social and political relations of two races of nearly equal numbers, from different quarters of the globe, and the most opposite of all others in every particular that distinguishes one race of men from another." Men in this sociology of slavery spoke for their womenfolk, in a kind of imposed chivalry. "Emancipation would destroy these relations—would divest the masters of their property, and subvert the relation, social and political that has existed between the races from almost the first settlement of the southern states."[38]

From comments like these, one would assume that Calhoun spoke for a traditional society in which change itself was the enemy and long-established social and political relations dominated the thinking of the master class. In fact, the slave South was a giant agricultural factory turning out hundreds of millions of dollars' worth of rice, tobacco, cotton, and sugar for the world market every year. The planters were forward-looking capitalists, reinvesting their profits in new lands and new techniques. Their society was not traditional but very modern—except for slavery.[39]

The final justification for slavery was not moral or social but a biological imperative. "As great as these disasters would be, they are nothing compared to what must follow the subversion of the existing relation between the two races. . . . Under this relation the two races have long lived in peace and prosperity." People of African ancestry were biologically suited, indeed biologically predetermined, to serve a master race. "While the European race has rapidly increased in wealth and numbers . . . the African race has multiplied, with not less rapidity, accompanied by great improvement, physically and intellectually, and the enjoyment of a degree of comfort with which the laboring class in few countries can compare, and confessedly greatly superior to what the free people of the same race possess in the non-slaveholding states. It may, indeed, be safely asserted, that there is no example in history in which a savage people, such as their ancestors were when brought into the country, have ever advanced in the same period so rapidly in numbers and improvement. . . . Social and political equality between them is impossible. No power on earth can overcome the difficulty. The causes resisting lie too deep in the principles of our nature to be surmounted."[40]

Setting aside the modern scholarly debates over the extent of slave breeding (i.e., the degree to which masters encouraged slave women to have children) and over whether slaves ate better and were housed better than first-generation free industrial laborers, Calhoun's claims of slave treatment were widely repeated by southern members of Congress and rejected by antislavery members. Calhoun's casual and pervasive racism, based on the idea that the European was a member of the ruling race and Africans were by nature inferior and meant for hard labor, was widely shared by whites in both North and South. Note that Calhoun did not take into account the views of the slaves. Whether the southerners believed his claims or not, there was ample evidence that slaves did not. Calhoun did not concern himself with such evidence, nor did other senators who regarded slavery as a positive good.[41]

Led by Calhoun, the upper house would adopt a policy parallel to the gag rule. Each petition would be received and then automatically referred to committee, forestalling the opportunity for antislavery senators to make a speech in support of the petition. The procedure did not have to be renewed at the start of each session, as the Senate proceeded by custom and this was now its custom.[42]

The gag-rule debates, however, had woken a sleeping tiger, who saw a threat to freedom of speech, press, and petition. John Quincy Adams, of Massachusetts, to whom a number of the petitions were sent, now wanted to know whether Congress had gagged him. It would seem, at first glance, that nothing could be farther from the grass-roots radical abolitionist movement than the privileges of freedom of speech of an elite public figure claimed in Congress. The connection was clear in hindsight, however. It was the free speech of the abolitionists that opponents in the North and South threatened. Mobs disrupting abolitionist meetings in Philadelphia, Boston, and elsewhere in free states and burning abolitionist literature in slave states violently denied the rights of the abolitionists. Using force to drive abolitionists from meeting halls and breaking into post offices to seize and destroy abolitionist writings were commonplace. The acts were praised by members of Congress. In 1836, Senator Thomas Hart Benton of Missouri praised the mobs for "silencing the gabbling tongues of female dupes and disper[sing] the assemblies" of the abolitionist "fanatics and visionaries." He did not mention the First Amendment. Following Adams's lead, the abolitionists made free speech "a rallying cry." As the American Anti-Slavery Society executive board had announced in 1835, "We never intend to surrender the liberty of press, of speech, or of conscience." Adams's high dudgeon on the floor of the House might have reflected his sense of his own importance rather than genuine camaraderie with the abolitionists, but the gag-rule debates brought them together.[43]

2

"Am I Gagged?"

NEITHER HOUSE OF CONGRESS'S resolutions quieted the debate over reception of the petitions. Instead, they had the opposite effect, because the means of prohibiting reception was a gag rule. The prospect of muzzling the members of the House, preventing them from speaking on an issue of importance in the House chamber, aroused the ire of John Quincy Adams. Adams's motives in entering the debate, unintentionally becoming its storm center, may never be fully understood. A man of almost rigid integrity, he kept public displays of his emotions to a minimum, though his diary revealed a man of passionate and strident opinions. A former president of the United States whose return to public life as a congressman from Massachusetts had made him an elder statesman of the republic, he was one of the few remaining links to the generation of the founders. As ambassador to Great Britain and later as secretary of state, he had argued with great force and ingenuity for Britain to pay slaveholders for the bondmen the Royal Navy had carried away after the War of 1812. Even then, he had conceded that "certainly a living, sentient being, and still more a human being, was to be regarded in a different light from the inanimate matter of which other private property might consist." When the slave ship *Antelope* was captured and the fate of its one hundred slaves was brought into American courts in 1825, he urged Attorney General William Wirt, arguing for the slaves' freedom (at the time the attorney general could maintain a private practice), to moderate his tone. Adams was not an abolitionist; indeed, he viewed the rise of the abolitionist movement with a certain realistic detachment. He thought slavery an abomination, but he had little use for radical abolitionist plans. Over the course of the gag-rule debates, he would express his antislavery views in increasingly strong language. Historians disagree about whether that shift was rooted in his animosity against the Jacksonian Democrats of the South or the evolution of his views on slavery. This essay argues that what appeared to be his shifting position was a result of the contingent logic of the debate itself.[1]

In 1835, the British had introduced their new policy of gradual emancipation in the West Indies, a subject that especially interested Adams, as he had been the US secretary of state from 1817 through 1825. In 1835, Garrison had invited the British abolitionist George Thompson to lecture in Boston. Adams took note of Thompson's visit. "There is an Englishman by the name of Thompson, lately come over from England, who is travelling about the country, holding meetings and making eloquent inflammatory harangues, preaching the immediate abolition of slavery. The general disposition of the people here is averse to these movements, and Thompson has several times been routed by popular tumults. But in some places he meets favorable reception and makes converts." Adams connected the abolitionist endeavor to events outside of New England, the same connection that southern congressmen assayed. In other words, he was not yet unsympathetic to their concerns, although he did not regard slavery as a positive good for them any more than for the slave. "There has been recently an alarm of slave insurrection in the State of Mississippi, and several white persons have been hung by a summary process of what they call Lynch's law; that is, mob law. Add to all this the approach of the Presidential election, and the question whether the President of the United States shall be a slave-holder or not." At the same time, he thought that southern overreaction to challenges to slavery could become a divisive issue in itself. "They never fail to touch upon this key in the South, and it has never yet failed of success. Rouse in the heart of the slave-holder the terror of his slave, and it will be a motive with him paramount to all others never to vote for any man not a slave-holder like himself."[2]

Though painfully aware of the debilities acquired over his nearly seventy years of active service for his country, he was especially concerned that the

John Quincy Adams was the first president to have his picture taken. This image, taken at his home in Quincy, Massachusetts, by Philip Haas in 1843, captures something of the gravity of the man, although photographic equipment at the time required the sitter to remain still for a good long while. Courtesy of Library of Congress.

voices of his fellow New Englanders might be muzzled by Hammond's resolution. Adams was not a powerbroker in the Whig Party—indeed, he stood apart from, and believed himself above, the conflict between the Democratic and Whig Parties—but privately and then publicly he began a campaign against the gag rule as an unconstitutional imposition on the rights of citizens and their representatives. With the gag-rule debate emerging, he confided to his diary on the December 26, 1835: "Harassed excessively with my own reflections upon the proposed new rule for the transaction of business in the House, upon which I grow disheartened as I proceed, and consider what I ought to say, but what it will probably be of no avail if I do say it. My mind is oppressed beyond what it ever was before, between a sense of public duty to take a bold and independent stand, and the almost certainty of being overpowered and broken down in the operation."[3]

When the House once again sat, on January 12, 1836, Adams was still unsure what to do. Fearing that no action on his part would suffice, seeing all manner of evils from every action, he elected a middle course: "As the petitioners had thought proper to send their petition to me, I wished to be able to inform them what disposition of it has been made by the House."[4]

For a time, Adams could not take any real part in the debate, as swelling in his legs prevented him from attending Congress. He returned to find the issue tucked away in the Pinckney committee. When Adams attempted to enter the discussion, the Speaker of the House, James K. Polk of Tennessee, Jackson's heir apparent, refused to give Adams the floor. Adams waited with increasing frustration as the House voted to excise the last part of the resolution, which conceded that the petitioners were decent folk. "I rose . . . but I was called with great vociferation to order, and not permitted to proceed."[5]

The progression of Adams's thinking cannot be fairly judged from the official record of the debates, but fortunately for students of his role in the debates, he fashioned a kind of shadow record of them in his diary. His thinking was evolving, not in a linear fashion, steadily embracing a more thoroughgoing antipathy to slavery, but in a series of small leaps. As he sought ways to protect the constitutional right of petition against what had become arguments for slavery, he began to adopt portions of the abolitionist position.

At first, Adams assayed a procedural approach, engaging in a running commentary with the Speaker and other members over House rules past and present. Nothing could fully silence Adams's voice on the floor even if he had to shout over other members. For example, when the Pinckney report was debated, Adams wanted a letter from Martin Van Buren on the subject read. Van Buren was running for the presidency, and although he supported the gag rule, the letter exonerated the petitioners' motives and character. Virginia representative John Robertson refused Adams's request. Speaking for the Pinckney committee, on which he served, he explained to the House why the committee resolution should not include anything complimentary about the petitioners. Robertson saw through Adams's ploy. Reading the letter aloud was equivalent to putting the final passage, on the petitioners' good will, on record, because the words of the letter would be entered into the *Register of Debates*. Adams persisted. "He was exceedingly anxious to have that part [of Van Buren's letter] read." Robertson, speaking for other proslavery members of the committee, spent nearly an hour explaining why he would not read the letter, including that it was too long to be read (although reading it would have taken about ten minutes). Finally, Robertson conceded the point, read the whole letter, and then disparaged it.[6]

In response, Adams asked for permission to speak, whereupon he was told that another member, George Owens of Georgia, had the floor. When Adams asked whether Owens would allow him to speak, Owens, who had graciously allowed Robertson to ramble on for more than an hour, curtly denied Adams's request. Apparently the civility that one southern member accorded to another stopped at the Mason-Dixon line.[7]

Adams then lost his patience. The resolution was unconstitutional, he shouted from his desk, to no effect. Was he gagged? he continued, giving the debate its popular name. No one answered. He then commenced a guerrilla war against the gag rule. He questioned the accuracy of clerk Walter Franklin's record of the vote on the resolution. It seemed to be 117 in favor and 68 against, but two members, Wise of Virginia and Thomas Glascock of Georgia, had refused to vote on it. Adams insisted that the record reflect their refusal rather than simply noting that they had not voted. As a result, the rest of May 26 was taken up with Speaker Polk, Adams, Wise, and Glascock going over the previous day's events. "Great disorder ensued," the clerk noted, as he valiantly tried to record their conversation. He had to put it in the record, lest Adams once again challenge its accuracy. This awkward merry-go-round was Adams's way of prolonging debate on the resolution by proxy after Owens and Polk refused to let him speak to the resolution itself.[8]

Adams was much in demand in Massachusetts as a speaker at public events, but he was not the orator that Hammond or Calhoun was: he lacked the former's passion and the latter's fierce commitment to a single cause. The Old Man of the Republic was formidable in other ways, however. He was a parliamentary bruiser, a bare-knuckle fighter in a room full of gentlemen. He had a deep strain of moral self-certitude, and he was indefatigable once set in his course. "My voice is now gone; my eyes are in no better condition," he recorded in his diary on July 27, but as long as he could walk to the Capitol, he was determined to be heard.[9]

Throughout these early stages of the gag-rule debates Adams was not a believer in the more thoroughgoing versions of emancipation, as he told a delegation from various Pennsylvania abolition societies calling on him in Philadelphia on his way home from Congress. "I desired them to return my thanks to their respective societies of the honor they had done me by these resolutions and to assure them of the grateful sentiments with which I received them . . . and I gave them a full and candid exposition of my own principles and views with regard to the institution of domestic slavery, differing from theirs under a sense of the compact and comprise in the Constitution of the United States. . . . I believed the cause itself would be more benefitted by such service as I could render to it by the discharge of my duty in Congress."[10]

In this diary entry, Adams acceded to a weak version of states'-rights theory in which the Union was conceived to be a compact or contract among the various sovereign states. John C. Calhoun had proposed this theory in various forms during the Nullification Crisis of 1828–33, and it reappeared in his defense of the gag rule. Senator John Ruggles of Maine, a lawyer and state politician who had won election to the US Senate as a Jacksonian Democrat, offered a version of this doctrine in the Senate on April 8, 1836. Calhoun then commended Ruggles and Maine for their patriotism. The memorial from the state legislature, Ruggles's comments, and Calhoun's compliment were widely reprinted in southern newspapers:

> That the U.S. government is a government of enumerated, limited, and defined powers, all of which are set forth in the Constitution, and that all powers, not granted, are reserved to the states and the people. That the power of regulating slavery within the confines of a state, was not granted, and therefore does not exist in the general government. . . .
> Mr. Ruggles said that these resolves were adopted in consequence of various resolves forwarded [to the Maine legislature] by various executives of N. Carolina, S. Carolina, Georgia, and Alabama. That they were passed by nearly unanimous votes by both houses and what was worthy of example, without a single word of debate.

The implied rebuke to Adams, who wanted to debate the antislavery petitions, was as obvious to readers as it was to the members of the Senate. As well, Ruggles was attempting to show that Jacksonian Party allegiance and Jacksonian ideas of states' rights trumped any sectional differences on slavery. Then as now, party unity sometimes overcame personal scruples. Adams did not agree with Calhoun or the Maine legislature that any state had the right to nullify a federal law that the state legislators did not like. Nor did he agree with Ruggles and Calhoun that the federal government lacked the authority to legislate within its enumerated (i.e., specifically granted) powers under the Constitution or that the federal government could violate the First Amendment rights of its citizens. As the Maine state legislature's resolutions and Ruggles's comments demonstrated, in 1836 Adams's views were not shared by all northern politicians, much less by members from the southern states.

Writing in his diary more than a year later, he doubted that "there are five members in the House who would vote for a bill to abolish slavery in the District of Columbia at this time."[11]

The rise of a Whig Party in opposition to Jackson's Democrats meant that Adams might gain some allies. In the 1836 election, Whigs won seats in Congress, but the presidency went to New York's Van Buren, Jackson's vice president. There was, moreover, little evidence that the abolitionist postal campaign had influenced national politics, much less that it was a force to be reckoned with in national politics. Given the election results, one might have expected the gag-rule controversy to pass into quietude as had the Missouri-statehood debates. But the abolitionists in Congress refused to acquiesce. When Speaker Polk called the second session of the Twenty-Fourth Congress to order, they were ready to present more petitions praying the end of slavery in the District of Columbia, presentations that would force a renewal of the debate over a gag rule.

It was the lame-duck session of the Twenty-Fourth Congress. According to the Constitution, the newly elected congress did not convene until later in the year. The old Congress met from December through the new year. In 1933 the Twentieth Amendment to the Constitution changed the rule, so that the new Congress comes into session on the third of January and the president, instead of being inaugurated at the beginning of March, is sworn into office at the beginning of January.

Perhaps it would not be necessary to reintroduce the gag rule in the lame-duck session, as the Pinckney resolution of May 1836 would still stand. On December 26, 1836, Adams tried to introduce a petition against slavery in the District. Representative Francis Pickens, a future governor of Confederate South Carolina, objected. Had not the issue been decided in May? Polk, still sitting in the Speaker's chair, ruled that the vote on the Pinckney resolution no longer bound the members. When Adams's attempt to read the petition was nevertheless objected to, he responded that "it appeared to him that the decision of the House at the last session went quite far enough to suppress the right of petition of the citizens of this country, and quite far enough to suppress the freedom of speech." But the motion not to receive any petition "went one step further. It went to settle the principle that petitions . . . should not even be received, and that, too, directly in the face of the Constitution itself." Adams's focus remained on the constitutional question, and the rights he defended were not those of the slaves but those of the free petitioners. "He hoped the people of this country would not tamely submit to the injustice and wrong which would be inflicted upon them by their immediate representatives, in deciding that their petitions should not be received."[12]

Adams was appealing not only to the House, indeed not primarily to the House (for its majority had already shown its disposition on the matter), but to popular opinion. He knew that popular opinion in the North did not favor abolition. One abolitionist editor, Elijah Lovejoy, was killed by an antiabolitionist mob in Alton, Illinois, at the same time that Adams was meeting with the delegation of Pennsylvania abolitionists. But Adams hoped that opinion on the right to petition would shift votes in the House in the next election cycle.[13]

Adams also knew that newspaper editors sat in the gallery. He was more than passingly acquainted with them and expected them to report his words, along with selections from the *Register of Debates*, in their papers. With the advent of cheaper newspapers after the invention of the rotary press, followed by the introduction of the daily newspaper, public opinion had become even more important in politics, a fact that Adams also knew. Newspaper editors made little effort to hide their own partisanship. They could be powerful allies of politicians. Jackson's most effective supporters were the newspaper editors Amos Kendall and Francis Preston Blair. Adams himself did not have particularly good working relations with the editors, complaining in Congress at one point that the papers had heaped "abuse and invective on me," but he read them and they covered his speeches.[14]

By appealing directly to the people in this fashion, Adams seems to have reversed his earlier decision not to give public addresses on the gag rule. There may have been another reason for this, however. A public talk might have opened Adams to the charge of being a partisan in the slavery debate, whatever he happened to say. Adams wanted to be the elder statesman who stood above the fray of partisanship. As John Greenleaf Whittier wrote in his introductory remarks to Adams's 1837 letter to his constituents, "John Quincy Adams belongs to neither of the prominent political parties, fights no partisan battles, and cannot be prevailed upon to sacrifice truth and principle upon the altar of party expediency and interest." Certainly, by appealing to the Constitution rather than taking a position on the substantive issue of slavery, Adams hoped to present his arguments as nonpartisan. He was speaking for the Constitution, not for any party, lobbying group, or faction. His achievements as a diplomat and then as secretary of state entitled him to the sobriquet "statesman," and, in a period when life expectancy was barely fifty years, his three score and ten entitled him to be regarded as an elder. But his notion of himself as a defender of constitutional order did not derive from his achievements or his reputation alone. It was an expression of his view of himself. As he wrote before the beginning of the lame-duck session on another, related matter, the defense of his father's reputation, "I have concluded that there is a duty for me to perform—a duty to the memory of my father; a duty to the character of the people of New England; a duty to truth and justice. If controversy is made, I shall have an arduous and . . . a very unthankful task to perform, and may sink under it. . . . I pray for temper, moderation, firmness, and self-control; and above all for a pure and honest purpose."[15]

That sense of purpose, expressed in Adams's attempt to introduce more than one hundred petitions against slavery in the District, contrary to the gag rule, led to a spontaneous and abortive attempt to censure Adams on February 6, 1837. His own account of it, along with a speech he delivered on that date, was published in Boston as *Letters from John Quincy Adams to His Constituents of the Twelfth Congressional District in Massachusetts. To which is added his speech in Congress, delivered February 9, 1837,* as well as in the *Register of Debates.* "Mr. Adams . . . stated that he had in his possession a paper on which he wished to have the opinion of the speaker. The paper came from twenty persons declaring themselves to be slaves. He wished to know whether the paper came under [the gag rule]."[16]

The paper purported to be the work of slaves. Thus Adams knew that his request for a ruling was tantamount to asking Polk, a slave owner himself, whether slaves had any of the rights of persons guaranteed in the Bill of Rights, in particular the right to petition for grievances. Note that the First Amendment provision for the right to petition uses the terms "the right of the people." If slaves were property only, such a claim would make no sense. But everyone knew that slaves were people—"other such persons," as described by the Constitution in the Three-Fifths Clause. Raising the question was enough to raise the hackles of the southern members. But Adams was not done. When Polk said that he would have to read it (to himself) in order to rule on it, "Adams said that if he sent it to the chair it would be in the possession of the house, whereas he wished to know of the speaker whether it fell under the [gag] rule before he presented it. The paper [i.e., the petition] purported to be from slaves, and this was one of those cases which it had occurred to his own mind was an imposition. The paper was signed partly by persons who could not write, they having made their mark, and partly by persons, judging from their writing, of little education. He would send the paper to the chair."[17]

Congress had received petitions from Native Americans signed only with their marks. The signers were not citizens of the United States, but they were people. Not only had those petitions been received but they had been read and then referred to a committee. Adams knew of this precedent for receiving a writing in such a form. It was the supposed authors of the current petition that were the cause of the uproar. He knew it would bring down the wrath of the House on him, but it was the only way to bring the petition question before a Congress that did not want to hear it. Charles E. Haynes, a Jacksonian from Georgia, was the first to take the bait. "He was astonished at the course pursued by the gentleman from Massachusetts, not only on this day, but on every petition day for some weeks since, but his astonishment had reached a height which he could not express when the gentleman rose and asked leave to present a paper purportedly coming from slaves."[18]

Haynes was followed by Dixon Lewis, of Alabama, who asked Haynes not to debate with Adams, as no southern gentleman "would either argue or vote upon the question," then proceeded to argue it. "He thought that representatives of the slaveholding states should demand that the attempt to introduce such a petition should instantly put in requisition the power of the house to punish the member." He did not mean that the House should punish Haynes or himself for debating reception, of course, but that the House should censure Adams for abusing the rules (i.e., the gag rule) against presenting the petition.[19]

While southern representatives were trying to top one another's indignation, Adams continued to agitate. He tried to present a petition from "nine ladies of the town of Fredericksburg." John Mercer Patton, whose district in Virginia had at one time included Fredericksburg, joined in the chorus calling for Adams's censure, but he admitted to having read the petition (he sat next to Adams in the chamber) and denounced the signers as women of ill repute. Waddy Thompson, of South Carolina, then formally moved that Adams be censured, at which motion members (according to the clerk) cried out loudly in favor of the motion. (Whether the clerk should have included the shouting without naming the shouters is another matter.) But members were not satisfied with Thompson's language. They wanted the reason for the censure to appear in the record, so Dixon Lewis supplied it: "That [Adams] by his attempt to introduce into this house a petition by slaves for the abolition of slavery in the district of Columbia committed an outrage on the rights and feelings of a large portion of the people of this Union; a flagrant contempt on the dignity of this house, and by extending to slaves, a privilege only belonging to freemen, directly incites the slave population to insurrection, and that the said member be forthwith called to the bar of the House, and be censured by the Speaker."[20]

Lewis's fear that submitting the petition would lead to slave insurrection was a little farfetched, but similar fears had led mobs in southern cities to break into post offices and destroy suspected abolitionist mail. Or perhaps the outrage he cited was less felt by the white population of the South, the vast majority of whom had no idea what Adams was doing, than by Lewis and his comrades in Congress. In any case, Adams's answer was as cool as Lewis's accusation was hot:

> The resolution charged him with attempting to present a petition from slaves for the abolition of slavery. He had not attempted to present a petition of the description at all. He had risen in his place and stated to the speaker that he had in his possession a paper from persons representing themselves to be slaves, but he had not stated what the object of it was, or what its prayer was, and he had asked the speaker whether, if he presented this paper, it would be included under the general order of the house [on the petitions] and be laid upon the table [i.e., tabled, without further discussion, as the order or motion to table something was not debatable] accordingly, and he meant to have the decision of the House [i.e., the ruling of the Speaker] before he proceeded one step further. . . .
>
> As to the fact in relation to the prayer of the petition, he would simply state to the gentleman from Alabama [Lewis] who had assumed, and sent to the clerk's table [the clerk sat at a table below the Speaker's desk] a resolution importing that the petition was for the abolition of slavery, this gentleman was mistaken, because it was the very reverse of this. . . .
>
> If the gentleman was about to press his motion, and the House was about to adopt it, they would be under the necessity of seeing what the paper was, and to that he would willingly submit. He would be willing the petition should be received and considered. And he would be willing for almost anything except to grant the prayer of this petition, because the gentleman from Alabama might find that its prayer was precisely what he had been so strenuously contending for.

In short, the paper was a hoax to show how little respect Lewis and other southern members had for freedoms enumerated in the First Amendment. Aware that they had been hornswoggled, the supporters of the censure motion tried to amend it, but much as they twisted and turned, they could not frame a resolution to censure Adams without embarrassing themselves. For a week the House wrangled, and the movement finally came to naught.[21]

Adams had succeeded in one respect: now the issue before the House was the freedom of speech of its members and whether speech offensive to other members was subject to censure. It was an old and much-honored parliamentary rule that what was said on the floor of the House of Commons was privileged. It could not be the basis for criminal or civil suits against the member. The House of Representatives had a similar rule, laid out in article 1, section 6, of the Constitution: "For any speech or debate in either house, [members] shall not be questioned in any other place." But article 1, section 5, clause 2, provided that "each House may determine the Rules of its Proceedings, punish its Members for disorderly Behavior, and, with the Concurrence of two thirds, expel a member." If John Quincy Adams's request to the Speaker was subject to censure or worse, then anyone who said anything or spoke in favor of saying anything that offended a majority of the House faced censure or worse. Representative Robertson, no friend to the abolitionist cause, would not go so far even to prevent speech that was antislavery. He told the House, "I have yet to learn that members of Congress may be proceeded against criminally for intimating or uttering opinions here which a majority may consider heretical or odious." In the end, only twenty-two votes for censure were registered, but the gag rule remained in place.[22]

On March 4, 1837, the newly elected president, Martin Van Buren, addressed the attendees at his inaugural. He warned against those in or out of government undermining "domestic institutions which, unwisely disturbed, might endanger the harmony of the whole." His meaning was clear to all. But if high-sounding generality would not suffice, he made the point even clearer by repeating a portion of the letter he had sent to the House in the spring of 1836. In his speech, Van Buren recognized the dangers of bringing the slavery debate to the center of national politics. Sectional discord could easily lead to the breakup of a union of free and slave states. "The last, perhaps the greatest, of the prominent sources of discord and disaster supposed to lurk in our political condition was the institution of domestic slavery." Van Buren then assayed a form of policy analysis that would become a commonplace of American political rhetoric, an appeal to the founding fathers. "Our forefathers were deeply impressed with the delicacy of this subject, and they treated it with a forbearance so evidently wise that in spite of every sinister foreboding it never until the present period disturbed the tranquility of our common country." As a rhetorical device, the appeal was effective; as history, it was nonsense. Disagreements over slavery had erupted during the Constitutional Convention, paralyzed Congress in the Missouri-statehood controversy, and reappeared over the question of the annexation of the new Republic of Texas. Van Buren knew the lesson he wanted to derive from history, however, and facts were not going to deter him. "Such a result is sufficient evidence of the justice and the patriotism of their course; it is evidence not to be mistaken that an adherence to it can prevent all embarrassment from this as well as from every other anticipated cause of difficulty or danger."[23]

The appeal to the authority of the founding fathers did make sense in one context. Originalism, the theory that constitutional provisions should be interpreted and applied according to the framers' purpose, is still a staple of constitutional jurisprudence. Van Buren's invocation of the founders' caution on the subject of slavery was not entirely wrong; they knew slavery was a time bomb and tried to diffuse it. They did not, however, think that their reticence would avert "all embarrassment" over slavery. In particular, John Adams expected that the time bomb would eventually explode if slavery did not end. As he wrote to George Churchman and Jacob Lindley on January 21, 1801, as he was preparing to leave Washington DC and the presidency, "The abolition of slavery must be gradual and accomplished with much caution and Circumspection. Violent means and measures would produce greater violations of Justice and Humanity, than the continuance of the practice." John Quincy Adams knew and shared his father's views.[24]

Van Buren's support of the gag rule was supposed to be a continuation of the founding fathers' approach: "Have not recent events made it obvious to the slightest reflection that the least deviation from this spirit of forbearance is injurious to every interest, that of humanity included?" The last phrase was a sop to the abolitionists: They were not bad men; they were misguided humanitarians. Oblivious to the political chaos their good intentions created, they pressed forward with their campaign. Van Buren then turned to his letter to the Pinckney committee regarding the reception of the petitions. Written during the presidential campaign, it was phrased so as not to offend the northern petitioners or the southern voters. Like Jackson, Van Buren

As shown in this 1858 portrait by George Alexander Peter Healy, Martin Van Buren hardly resembles the Sly Fox of Kinderhook, as he was known at the time of his election, but something in the depiction suggests that he was an astute politician. Courtesy of White House Portrait Collection.

realized that the only way to win the highest office was to get votes from both North and South. Indeed, the political party system of the period functioned to ensure that presidential candidates were as appealing to as many voters as possible.

> Perceiving before my election the deep interest this subject was beginning to excite, I believed it a solemn duty fully to make known my sentiments in regard to it, and now, when every motive for misrepresentation has passed away, I trust that they will be candidly weighed and understood. At least they will be my standard of conduct in the path before me. I then declared that if the desire of those of my countrymen who were favorable to my election was gratified, "I must go into the Presidential chair the inflexible and uncompromising opponent of every attempt on the part of Congress to abolish slavery in the District of Columbia against the wishes of the slaveholding States, and also with a determination equally decided to resist the slightest interference with it in the States where it exists."

Van Buren was clearly no friend to abolition, but as events would prove, particularly in his reluctance to annex the newly independent Republic of Texas, he was no friend to slavery either. He was, in short, a Free-Soiler, opposed to the expansion of slavery. None of this was yet apparent to his Democratic supporters in the South, though some, as they had shown when his letter was read, suspected that he did not care for their peculiar institution.[25]

Polk, reelected Speaker of the House at the start of the Twenty-Fifth Congress, was similarly determined to put the petition issue to rest. He had squeaked into that office by eight votes, evidence that some of his fellow congressmen did not like the way he had handled the censure movement. He himself had been "delighted" by the imposition of the gag rule but less than pleased with the way that imposition had turned out. In any case, he told the body that it would be "impossible for him to keep order unless supported by the House." It should be noted that he and Adams were formally cordial to one another throughout these sessions, Polk recognizing that Adams was the elder statesman, and when Adams died in 1848, then president Polk ordered all executive offices closed and the cessation of all business for two days.[26]

Polk's plea to the House to help him keep order fell on deaf ears. When on December 18, 1837, at the opening of the second session of the Twenty-Fifth Congress, William Slade once again rose during petition time and then began to read a speech calling for the abolition of slavery throughout the land, disorder erupted in the House. Members shouted objection after objection to Slade's continuing even though this session of the House had not yet agreed to a gag rule. Polk tried shouting above the din, to no avail. Slade continued to stand, though every sentence he tried to read was cut short by points of order and other privileged motions. According to Adams, the "slavers were at their wits' end." With the normal parliamentary rules effectually suspended and Slade continuing to speak, entire southern-state delegations marched out of the chamber. Finally, Polk found some ground to ask Slade to sit, which he did. When one southern legislator who remained moved for an adjournment, Adams, who had watched the circus quietly, reminded the Speaker that insufficient members remained to pass a motion to adjourn. Southerners grumpily reentered the chamber long enough to cast their votes to end the day's mischief.[27]

Perhaps a collateral attack would work to gain the ear of Congress to the substance of the petitions? Petitions against the admission of Texas to the Union contained condemnations of slavery. (Congress had not yet authorized the annexation; that would come with the lame-duck session of the Twenty-Sixth Congress in the winter of 1845.) The issue was joined in the second session, in February 1838, with a petition from the Vermont legislature against the admission of Texas. The petition contained language condemning slavery and expressing the fear that the admission of a new slave state would lead to the dissolution of the Union. The problem southern delegates had with the Vermont petition was compounded when Alabama's legislature petitioned Congress to admit Texas. If states were sovereign, and their legislative pronouncements reflected the will of their people, how could states'-rights men in Congress refuse to receive the Vermont memorial and receive the one from Alabama? Adams's diary showed that he relished the prospect: "a new day" had dawned. All of the petitions were referred to the Committee on Foreign Affairs. At last a petition that condemned slavery was received. But nothing came from the committee, and Texas was not annexed. Adams was a fighter, but sparring with the gag rule was like punching the tar-baby in the Chandler Harris's Uncle Remus story "The Tar-Baby": the harder one struck, the more one was stuck. But Adams kept on swinging.[28]

Holding Adams's coat in this fight was Theodore Dwight Weld, a periodic visitor to Washington and a peripatetic organizer of the petition movement. For the more that Congress tried to close the door, the harder the petitioners pushed against it. In the Twenty-Fifth Congress, Weld and his comrades arranged for more than 100,000 petitions, with more than a half million signatures (though many petitions were signed by the same men and women). In a sense, the increased energy of the petition campaign put almost insuperable pressure on Adams. Though he now had allies, his voice was still the one most heard in the House on petition days. On one day in February 1838, he offered more than 350 petitions against slavery.[29]

For their part, southern members had not grown resigned to Adams's and others' presentation of the antislavery petitions. The repetition of the debate over the gag rule had created a unity among southern members that had not existed previously. Calhoun had seen the need for such a step, writing to a private correspondent, "I fear there is not spirit enough in the Southern delegation to meet the crisis." The answer was to put aside party allegiance and any differences members from the Upper South states might have with those from the Lower South and form a phalanx of opposition to the reception of the petitions. The debates over the gag rule thus had the consequence, unanticipated by both sides, of making sectional rather than party affiliation the basis of members' position on the issue.[30]

After four years of debate over the gag rule, representatives from the South looked for a way to foreclose the debate over the acceptance of the petitions that arose with each new session. Finally, supporters of the gag rule found a solution. It was so easy that one wonders why they did not hit on it at the start, in December 1835. The House had standing rules. These included the provision for petition days before the formal session was called to order. Why not add to these standing rules one that rejected all petitions concerning slavery in the District? The new rule would not close the door to debate on slavery entirely, for the question of Texas's admission to the Union had yet to be decided, and consideration of that question would inevitably raise the slavery issue. But a proposal for an additional standing rule would go to the rules committee, a body created in the very first session of the House. It had a fixed number of representatives, chosen at the beginning of each session, divided in this period according to party affiliation. Until 1840 the debates over petitions took place before the selection of the members of the rules committee. This practical obstacle to a standing rule against reception of the petitions could be overcome if the committee made a rule retroactive. Waddy Thompson and Henry Wise were the authors of this idea. Adams saw what was about to happen and tried to divert the discussion, but on January 28, 1840 the House made the gag rule 21 (later rule 25) of its standing rules. Henceforth, at least in theory, anyone who tried to argue for reading or referring an antislavery petition was in violation of the House rules and subject to House discipline.

3

"He Knew That They All Abhorred Slavery"

ADAMS MIGHT HAVE HOPED that the election of 1840, with the Democratic incumbent Van Buren replaced by the Whig candidate, William Henry Harrison, would change the fortunes of the antislavery petitioners in Congress. But the Twenty-Sixth Congress had a small majority of Democratic members. Harrison passed away shortly after his inauguration, and Vice President John Tyler, of Virginia, as Adams knew, was no friend to antislavery. In any case, Adams had another opportunity to make the case against slavery. In this increasingly vitriolic climate of opinion, the antebellum federal courts heard a series of slave cases starting with *United States v. Libellants and Claimants of the Schooner Amistad* (1841) and ending with *Dred Scott v. Sanford* (1857). During the years between its inception and its resolution, the *Amistad* case was a subject of great public interest only surpassed in later years by the *Dred Scott* case. In June 1839 a Cuban schooner carrying fifty-three slaves sailed from Havana to another port on the island. Along the way, the slaves rose up, killed the captain, the cook, and other crew members and ordered the two planter-owners aboard to sail for Africa. Instead, they managed to bring the ship into US territorial waters, where it was boarded by American sailors who took it to the port of New London, Connecticut.[1]

The *Amistad* presented familiar issues both of salvage (i.e., who could legally benefit from the saved ship and cargo) and of the legality of the slave trade under international treaties. With regard to salvage, the question was whether the cargo of the ship—the Africans—belonged to the men who boarded (two naval officers) and took the ship into the American port, the Cuban owners, or the two Spanish men who in fact had purchased the majority of the slaves and who, after the uprising, were to have sailed the ship to Africa under the orders of the slaves. There were also questions of a crime at sea (the slaves had killed at least two crew members) and the jurisdiction of the federal court over the case. The district court over which Judge Andrew Judson presided referred the question of criminal jurisdiction to the circuit court. Sitting in the circuit court, Justice Smith Thompson, who hailed from New York, ruled that the district court had jurisdiction over the case in admiralty as a question of "salvage" but not over the alleged crimes at sea, as these belonged to the circuit court. The questions then became, who owned the ship and were the Africans slaves or free? The queen of Spain intervened in support of the Cuban owners, who were Spanish subjects, resting the case upon a maritime treaty between Spain and the United States ratified in 1821. As a question of salvage, the case was of little importance and could have ended in the district court with a decree that the ship be returned to its Cuban owners.[2]

The alleged slaves also petitioned for their freedom, arguing that they were free when the alleged slave traders kidnapped them and carried them from their African homeland to Cuba (violating Spanish law) before their transshipment on the *Amistad*. Justice Thompson found that the district court could also hear arguments on the detention of the slaves. For this reason, as a freedom suit, the case became a highly publicized and politicized one, closely watched by southern slave interests and northern abolitionists. At the circuit court preliminary hearing on habeas corpus writs for the incarcerated slaves, Justice Thompson had made clear his abhorrence of slavery but stated that he was bound by existing slave law. Did that law apply to the high seas? Van Buren's secretary of state, John Forsyth, a virulently proslavery Georgian, tried every trick to return the slaves to their owners by executive decree. But helped by abolitionists and ultimately represented by, among others, Adams (who had coauthored the treaty with Spain in 1819), the slaves' suit raised vital questions about the slave trade's legality, the morality of bondage, and the slaves' right to rebel.[3]

Supreme Court Justice Joseph Story of Massachusetts, shown here in a daguerreotype made in 1844, the year of his death, wrote the opinion for the court in the *Amistad* case. Story detested slavery but feared that abolitionism might destroy the Union. He thus wrote a narrow opinion based on international law rather than on the Constitution. He did incorporate some of Adams's views, however. Courtesy of Library of Congress.

Judge Judson, once again hearing the case, noted that Spain had outlawed the slave trade in 1817. He decreed that the alleged slaves were in fact free and should be turned over to the president of the United States to be returned to their homes in Africa. The circuit court concurred, Justice Thompson joining Judson. But the owners wanted the slaves, and the queen, with the support of Secretary of State Forsyth, appealed the circuit court ruling to the US Supreme Court. The Supreme Court had before it evidence that the human cargo were not Cuban slaves by birth and not simply en route from one Cuban port to another, but newly taken from Africa. What was more, the documents the ship's master carried were fraudulent, created to get around Spain's agreement with Great Britain not to trade in African slaves. A co-counsel for the slaves, Roger Baldwin, urged that "the American people have never imposed it as a duty on the government of the United States, to become actors in an attempt to reduce to slavery, men found in a state of freedom, by giving extra-territorial force to a foreign slave law. Such a duty would not only be repugnant to the feelings of a large portion of the citizens of the United States, but it would be wholly inconsistent with the fundamental principles of our government."[4]

For the United States, the queen of Spain, and the Cuban slave owners (remember that Cuba was a colony of Spain), US Attorney General Henry Gilpin made a simple argument: " If . . . the same law exists in regard to property in slaves as in other things; and if documentary evidence, from the highest authority of the country where the property belonged, accompanied with possession, is produced; it follows that the title to the ownership of this property is as complete as is required by law." Slaves were property under Spanish law; these were Spanish slaves aboard a Spanish ship. They must be returned to their owners. Gilpin was Van Buren's choice for the office of attorney general and served during Van Buren's entire tenure. Van Buren saw the case as an incendiary one and wanted to distance himself from it, as it had been in its early stages when he sought reelection. The easiest way to avoid turning the case into a cause célèbre was to return the slaves to their owners.[5]

This time, no one gagged Adams. He spoke not only as co-counsel for the slaves in the appeal but also as a former president, secretary of state, and scholar of international law. He ranged over two thousand years of legal learning, through many nations' case law and codes, and principles of international relations. He rehearsed the facts. While he knew that Justice Joseph Story, also from Massachusetts, hated slavery as much as he did, he could not know how any of the justices would respond. This, in a sense, was the speech on slavery he had always wanted to give in Congress, and this time he did not need to defend himself from the calumny of slaveholders. One should thus read his long and learned oral argument as part of the gag-rule debate, the full answer to those who would impose it on advocates for human freedom. "Old man eloquent," as he was sometimes derisively called behind his back, lived up to that name on this occasion. He knew that the oral argument before the Supreme Court would be published and widely read, and he poured into it a genuine sense of personal outrage:

I derive, in the distress I feel both for myself and my clients, consolation from two sources—first, that the rights of my clients to their lives and liberties have already been defended by my learned friend and colleague [Baldwin] in so able and complete a manner as leaves me scarcely anything to say, and I feel that such full justice has been done to their interests, that any fault or imperfection of mine will merely be attributed to its true cause; and secondly, I derive consolation from the thought that this Court is a Court of JUSTICE. And in saying so very trivial a thing, I should not on any other occasion, perhaps, be warranted in asking the Court to consider what justice is. Justice . . . is *"The constant and perpetual will to secure to every one HIS OWN right."* This observation is important, because I appear here on the behalf of thirty-six individuals, the life and liberty of every one of whom depend on the decision of this Court. The Court, therefore, I trust, in deciding this case, will form no lumping judgment on these thirty-six individuals, but will act on the consideration that the life and the liberty of every one of them must be determined by its decision for himself alone.[6]

Adams was responding here to the claim that slaves were not persons and thus had no right to petition Congress, made by Congressman Lewis and others in Congress four years earlier. On this occasion, the supposed slaves who were petitioning for their freedom in the highest federal court in the land were being heard, a comparison that Adams implied rather than stated. By insisting that the individual slaves had rights as individuals, he was making the larger point that all men had rights in their own right, not because governments classified them by color or ancestry.

Adams had other targets besides racial prejudice and unfair laws. He knew that he was taking on the executive branch of the government, in particular former president Martin Van Buren. "When I say I derive consolation from the consideration that I stand before a Court of Justice, I am obliged to take this ground, because, as I shall show, another Department of the Government of the United States has taken, with reference to this case, the ground of utter injustice, and these individuals for whom I appear, stand before this Court, awaiting their fate from its decision, under the array of the whole Executive power of this nation against them, in addition to that of a foreign nation." Ironically, Van Buren was no longer president when the case came before the high court and would shortly become a standard-bearer of the Free-Soil Party, a political coalition determined to prevent the spread of slavery into the western territories of the United States. Free-Soilers like Van Buren did not abandon their racist prejudices, however. Still, Adams had never had much use for Van Buren, and Van Buren's stance against the petitions had given Adams one more occasion to distrust the president. Here was a chance for some payback. "It is, therefore, peculiarly painful to me, under present circumstances, to be under the necessity of arraigning before this Court and before the civilized world, the course of the existing Administration in this case. But I must do it. That Government is still in power, and thus, subject to the control of the Court, the lives and liberties of all my clients are in its hands." For Van Buren's administration and Secretary of State Forsyth only displayed "sympathy with the white, antipathy to the black."[7]

Secretary of State Forsyth had a role to play in Adams's morality play as a proxy for Lewis, Haynes, Robertson, Thompson, and all the others "outraged" when Adams had tried to present a petition from slaves. A former US representative and senator from Georgia, Forsyth was a defender of slavery in both houses of Congress and a slave owner himself. Although he had had no direct part in the imposition of the gag rule, Adams treated him as a stand-in for those who had: "This sympathy with Spanish slave-traders is declared by the Secretary [Forsyth]. . . . The sympathy of the Executive government, and as it were of the nation, in favor of the slave-traders, and against these poor, unfortunate, helpless, tongueless, defenceless Africans." Adams's depiction of the slaves was condescending—he did not believe that they were the equal of the white man in anything but their rights in a court of law—but his racism was mild compared with that of the gag-rule gang. And his sympathy was plainly with "the men who had restored themselves to freedom, and secured their oppressors to abide the consequences of the acts of violence perpetrated by them."[8]

Abolition could not be mentioned in the House of Representatives because, as Congressman Lewis explained, it might lead to slave rebellion. Here was a slave rebellion in the flesh. Adams's defense of the *Amistad* blacks suggested that rebellion in the name of personhood and personal freedom might be a form of justice. Had he even implied as much on the floor of the house, he might well have been censured in 1837. In the Supreme Court chamber, but one floor beneath the two houses, such a proposition was far safer. The Spanish minister was greatly heartened by what he heard from the Senate debates on the *Amistad*. "The minister refers with great apparent satisfaction to certain resolutions of the Senate, adopted at the instance of Mr. [John C.] Calhoun . . . as follows: 1. 'Resolved—That a ship or vessel on the high seas, in time of peace, engaged in a lawful voyage, is according to the laws of nations under the exclusive jurisdiction of the state to which her flag belongs as much as if constituting a part of its own domain.' 2. 'Resolved—That if such ship or vessel should be forced, by stress of weather, or other unavoidable cause into the port, and under the jurisdiction of a friendly power, she and her cargo, and persons on board, with their property, and all the rights belonging to their personal relations, as established by the laws of the state to which they belong, would be placed under the protection which the laws of nations extend to the unfortunate under such circumstances.'" Recall that the Senate had its own gag rule, the work of the same John C. Calhoun, and reference to his draft of the Senate resolution tied Adams's brief even closer to the gag-rule controversy. Adams rightly supposed that Calhoun was following the arguments, as Calhoun prepared for the Senate two resolutions supporting Van Buren's handling of the case and Adams, in the House, prepared resolutions condemning the president's position. Calhoun's resolutions passed; Adams's did not.[9]

Adams had one more argument to make against any reading of the Treaty of 1819 between Spain and the United States that required the United States to return the *Amistad* prisoners to their Spanish owners. It was based on a special kind of authority, the eyewitness: he was there at the creation of the treaty; he helped write it; "I will speak of my own knowledge, for it happened that on the renewal of the Treaty [of commerce with Spain] the whole of the negotiations with the then minister of Spain passed through my hands, and I am certain that neither of us ever entertained an idea that this word merchandise was to apply to human beings. And the supposed slaves were human beings. . . . Is anything more absurd than to say these forty Africans are robbers, out of whose hands they have themselves been rescued? Can a greater absurdity be imagined in construction than this, which applies the double character of robbers and of merchandise to human beings?" It was this pervasive "double character" of slavery, that slaves were human beings treated by an absurd and demeaning law as things—merchandise—that the petitioners had protested.[10]

But slavery was legal under state and federal law. How was Adams to condemn the treatment of the *Amistad* prisoners without openly condemning

American law? Abolitionists like Garrison had no trouble doing this; in his view, laws that enslaved men and women were wrong and not to be obeyed. Adams had to steer a course closer to the language of the Constitution. "The [Constitution] recognizes that the slaves, held within some of the States of the Union, only in their capacity of persons—persons held to labor or service in a State under the laws thereof—persons constituting elements of representation in the popular branch of the National Legislature—persons, the migration or importation of whom should not be prohibited by Congress prior to the year 1808." This was the reading of the absence of the word *slave* from the Constitution and its replacement with *persons*, upon which the entire edifice of constitutional antislavery was built. If slaves were persons, rather than things, they had natural rights. These rights trumped the property rights conferred by state law. "The Constitution no where recognizes them as property. The words slave and slavery are studiously excluded from the Constitution. Circumlocutions are the fig-leaves under which these parts of the body politic are decently concealed. Slaves, therefore, in the Constitution of the United States are recognized only as persons, enjoying rights and held to the performance of duties."[11]

Finally, Adams had made clear where he stood on domestic slavery. It was not the same place as he stood in 1835. He once again pointed to the copy of Declaration of Independence framed above the Supreme Court bench and railed, "Has the expunging process of black lines passed upon these two Declarations of Independence in their gilded frames? Has the 4th of July, '76, become a day of ignominy and reproach?"[12]

Adams did not know it yet, but his opponents in the House were preparing another censure of him, this time not the impulse of a moment but a studied plan. In response, Adams would make the same arguments that he rehearsed here: that he stood with the founders, with America's ideals, and its history. But he had a clue to the cabal against him, a letter. Holding it, he brought the House chamber into the courtroom.

> I know not who is the author, but it appeared with that almost official sanction, on the day of meeting of this Court. It purports to be a review of the present case. The writer begins by referring to the decision of the District Court, and says the case is "one of the deepest importance to the southern states." I ask, may it please your Honors, is that an appeal to JUSTICE? What have the southern states to do with the case, or what has

the case to do with the southern states? The case, as far as it is known to the courts of this country, or cognizable by them, presents points with which the southern states have nothing to do. It is a question of slavery and freedom between foreigners; of the lawfulness or unlawfulness of the African slave trade; and has not, when properly considered, the remotest connection with the interests of the southern states. What was the purpose or intent of that article, I am not prepared to say, but it was evidently calculated to excite prejudice, to arouse all the acerbities of feeling between different sections of this country, and to connect them with this case, in such a manner as to induce this Court to decide it in favor of the alleged interests of the southern states, and against the suppression of the African slave trade.[13]

Adams did not intend to confine his own remarks to the African slave trade. He once again pointed to the copy of the Declaration of Independence that hung behind the justices' bench:

That DECLARATION says that every man is "endowed by his Creator with certain inalienable rights," and that "among these are life, liberty, and the pursuit of happiness." If these rights are inalienable, they are incompatible with the rights of the victor to take the life of his enemy in war, or to spare his life and make him a slave. If this principle is sound, it reduces to brute force all the rights of man. It places all the sacred relations of life at the power of the strongest. No man has a right to life or liberty, if he has an enemy able to take them from him. There is the principle. There is the whole argument of this paper.

Adams had turned his oral argument into a kind of generic petition, a petition of all petitions. It was received, he could speak to it, and in the end the high court rejected the appeal of the Spanish government, the slavers, the president, and the secretary of state and ordered that the *Amistad* prisoners be returned to their homeland as free persons.[14]

No sooner had Adams argued successfully for the *Amistad* Africans than the second attempted censure of Adams exploded in the House. It filled two weeks' pages of the 1842 *Congressional Globe*. Not surprisingly, Adams brought it on himself by ignoring the standing rule against presenting antislavery petitions. Adams's week-long speech in his defense, made off and on during a cold February from the second to the sixth, in which a seventy-five-year-old

tutored, harangued, and reminisced (replete with references to his association with earlier generations of Virginians, to wit, Washington, Jefferson, and
Madison). He knew, he told the House, that "they all abhorred Slavery." At the
end of the week, with petitions supporting him flooding the House, the movement to censure him simply fell apart, but the effort nearly killed him. Representative Joshua Giddings of Ohio, whose antislavery credentials were as
burnished as Adams, many years later recalled the events that he witnessed.

> In January, 1842, several citizens of Massachusetts got up a petition de-
> signed to test the sincerity of the slaveholders in their repeated threats
> to dissolve the Union. This was sent to Mr. Adams. He conversed about
> it to friends out of the House, and announced the course he intended to
> pursue. He had not the least hesitation as to his duty, and the manner in
> which he should perform it. The next day, when Massachusetts was called
> for petitions, in a clear and distinct voice he announced to the Speaker
> and the House that he held in his hand the petition of Benjamin Emerson
> and forty-five other citizens of Haverhill that Congress should take imme-
> diate measures to procure the peaceable dissolution of the Union, because
> nothing could be permanent that was not equitable; that instead of main-
> taining liberty, it sustained southern slavery, and, if it continued, must
> be overwhelmed by the judgment of Providence. There was then a scene
> thrilling through every heart in that hall, sublime beyond description.[15]

The friends with whom Adams had discussed the matter were abolitionists
like Theodore Dwight Weld, who was an unofficial lobbyist for the abolition
movement in Washington. A deputation of the antislavery congressmen met
with Adams, and it became clear that he intended once again to force the
hand of the slave-state representatives. On their part, the southern members
had once again caucused and decided upon their course of action. As it happened, the two sides had exactly the same idea: the censure of Adams. For
Adams, who would be given the floor to defend his conduct against such a
motion, now wanted to speak his mind. News of the impending clash had
spread through the town, and the galleries were filled with spectators, reporters, and Washington political players. The events of January 24, 1842, on the
floor of the House began with the petition in Adams's hand.

> A score of slaveholders were on their feet at once, trembling with rage.
> Mr. Holmes, of S. C., asked, Is it a petition to dissolve the Union? Mr.

Adams, without making a reply, moved to refer the petition to a select committee, with instructions to report against its prayer, and give the reasons for it. He did not indicate those reasons, but they were evident. Congress had no power to grant the request. Every one, in this excitement, paid strict attention to what was said by the Speaker and Mr. Adams. Mr. Hopkins, of Va., inquired if it was in order to move to burn the petition in the presence of the House? This only drew from Mr. Adams, in subsequent remarks, the soubriquet of the "combustible member," which he applied to Mr. Hopkins. Mr. Butler, of Tenn., moved to lay the petition on the table, and publish, in order that the people might understand its contents. Mr. Wise, of Va., inquired if it was in order to move a vote of censure upon the member presenting it? A few minutes after, Mr. Gilmer, of Va., a slaveholding Democrat . . . offered a resolution that, in presenting a petition for the dissolution of the Union, the member had incurred the just censure of the House.[16]

Adams knew that if a debate on the petition began, as its presenter he would be free to discuss it. It was a tactic of passive aggression he had used many times previously. For example, he had often badgered the Speaker for a ruling on whether he could present a petition, in the process putting the content of the petition on record, full well knowing that he would be told that the House had already ruled that such petitions must be rejected and that such presentations were out of order. On this occasion, he would, he said, of course oppose any petition to dissolve the Union, but he would also have the chance to explain the thinking of the signatories. If the members agreed to have it read, then Adams would had won the battle: a petition pertaining to slavery (whatever it actually said) would have been received and read. He hoped he had the gag-rule members on the horns of a dilemma. But they bulled ahead.

At this point, the House adjourned until the next morning [January 25]. The slaveholding members were in high spirits. They had in their grasp the man who had caused them so much trouble for four or five years, and possessed the power to crush him and avenge their injuries. That night, when darkness shrouded the capital and its streets were desolate, they held a convocation to consult how they should proceed in order to degrade and destroy him. To give character to this prosecution, they looked around for a Whig [i.e., a member of Adams's party] who would be likely to do their work for them. Mr. Marshall, of Kentucky, a nephew of Chief Justice Marshall, was selected to prosecute the revered patriot. . . . He had been a member of the Kentucky Legislature, and had there stood up nobly in defence of human rights. He was ambitious, and felt a desire to cross swords with the distinguished man of whom it was said that no man ever assailed him with impunity.[17]

Monday and Tuesday had been spent on the preliminaries. No other business occupied the House, which was a victory of sorts for Adams, as the fencing over the petition was a proxy for a debate over slavery. Another irony in a debate abounding in ironies was that Representative Marshall and others truly feared that any federal action against slavery would lead to the dissolution of the Union—with the South, not the North, leading the way. The southern bloc would have to rewrite its resolution. Adams had thus far held the slave-state members at bay, but Wednesday's session would bring him closer to public shaming if they had their way.

> The next morning, Mr. M. [Marshall] presented a substitute for the resolution of Mr. Gilmer, but the substance was the same. The preamble set forth that the presentation of the petition was an insult upon the people, disreputable to a representative, and that he [Adams] had committed high treason against the government. The resolutions declared that he justly deserved expulsion, but that, in consideration of the past services and reputation of the accused, the House, in its grace and mercy, was content with expressing its severe censure. . . . Mr. Marshall eloquently addressed the House, and enlarged upon the theme, arraigned the whole past life of Mr. Adams, so far as he had stood forth the champion of liberty, and when he had spoken against oppression, and set these things before the indignant body. He declared that he had committed high treason, and might be tried for that crime.[18]

Treason against the United States was the one crime precisely defined in the Constitution's article 2, section 3, clause 1: "Treason against the United States shall consist only in levying war against them, or in adhering to their enemies, giving them aid and comfort. No person shall be convicted of treason unless on the testimony of two witnesses to the same overt act, or on confession in open court." The House of Representatives was not such a court, however, nor could anyone have argued that Adams's conduct in the House amounted to treason under the constitutional definition. The House, of course, had the power, under article I, section 5, clause 2—"Each House may determine the rules of its proceedings, punish its members for disorderly behavior, and, with the concurrence of two-thirds, expel a member"—but Marshall and his allies were unlikely to be able to summon a two-thirds majority to expel Adams. Hence both Marshall's gracious offer not to seek Adams's expulsion and his reference to treason were nothing more than bombast.

> Mr. Adams had not risen to answer Mr. Gilmer. He had looked on the excitement of the previous day with a placid smile, as if something amusing was passing in his mind, as he saw the storm raging about him. Now, we who sat near could see the inmost workings of his soul written upon his countenance. God had given him a countenance upon which might be seen every serious emotion of his mind. He had no secrets on political matters, and no one ever could in plainer terms show what his sentiments were. Before Marshall had concluded, we could see the storm beginning to arise in his breast. The clouds began to gather, and we expected to see the tempest burst with overwhelming force.[19]

It was a commonplace of antebellum high culture that one could see evidence of a man's character, indeed of his soul, in his physical appearance. The face was thus the gateway to the soul. An entire pseudoscience, phrenology, mapped virtue and vice in the face and skull. Less prejudicially, early psychologists and poets agreed that "when the soul . . . is agitated, the human visage becomes a living picture." Phrenology was all the rage among American intellectuals, and George Combe, a Scottish lawyer, gave very popular lectures on the subject during a visit to the United States in 1839 and 1840. Adams knew about the lectures but was not a devotee of Combe's views. He "classed it with alchemy."

> When [Adams] arose, he was the "observed of all observers." Everyone expected him to reply. The Speaker's eye was fixed upon him. As he rose, dignity marked every movement; he was deliberate in language, and choice in his use of words. He said: "Mr. Speaker—It is no part of my design to reply to anything that has fallen from the gentleman in relation to myself. I will only say that, so far as his speech refers to high treason, the constitution defines that to be levying war against government—and it is not for him or his puny mind to define it." He then called upon the clerk

to read the first paragraph of the Declaration of Independence, down to the definition of rights and duties [the same theatrical device he had used in the *Amistad* argument]. He made this request in majestic terms three different times, at each repetition raising his voice and giving greater emphasis to his words. While he was repeating the request, the clerk had turned to the Declaration, and now commenced reading. He paused once before concluding the passage, and Mr. Adams, still standing, requested him to pass on to the clause declaring it to be the right and duty of the people to alter or abolish the government when it was found unsuited to their requirements. As the clerk closed the book, Mr. Adams repeated that it is our right and duty to alter or abolish the government when it becomes subversive of the undying truths on which it was founded. Sir, said he, if this House is capable of entertaining the resolution—if it entertains jurisdiction of such a question—I ask time to prepare my defence, and to show that the denial of the right of petition is in itself a grievance which justifies the resort to this right and duty. Mr. Cooper said that the gentleman from Massachusetts had mistaken the sense of the House if he supposed time would be given him to prepare his defence. Mr. Adams simply asked if a case was ever known that an accused person was denied time to prepare his defence—and compelled to proceed at once?[20]

Adams, a lawyer, was treating the proceeding as a trial. He had asked the Speaker and been granted time to defend himself "in a trial." In fact, it was not a trial, except in a metaphorical sense. Adams saw the basic rights of Americans, including the rights of members of the House, as being on trial. Representative Mark Cooper of Georgia had served in the House as a Whig, lost reelection in 1840, and returned in 1842 as a Democrat. He too was a lawyer, but he saw the matter as purely procedural. But the Speaker of the House, John White, a Kentucky Whig, allowed Adams the time he needed.

A motion was made to continue the prosecution, and postpone it one week; and that, in the meantime, the resolution be laid on the table and printed for information. Mr. Wise said that the motion to print was debatable, and at once took the floor. He had formerly engaged in a debate with Mr. Adams, and came out badly damaged by the collision. He saw that now he had an opportunity to assail his adversary to his heart's content, and Mr. Adams would have but brief opportunity to reply. He spoke two days, and ended by calling on the Democratic party to sustain the resolution of censure; for if they did not, slavery would be abolished, and the last remaining democratic institution destroyed . . . laughter followed the utterance of the sentiment in the House.[21]

John Wise's eagerness had betrayed him into a hasty generalization, but his contention was not as ludicrous as it appears today. Southern proslavery thought assumed that the only true democracy must be founded on slavery. Athenian democracy, which southern spokesmen often praised, had depended on both slavery and an overseas empire. In any case, without a better report of what Wise actually said, it is hard to dismiss it as nonsense. The *Register of Debates* had ceased publication, and the *Congressional Globe* did not offer verbatim reports of the speeches until 1851. "The withering reply of Mr. Adams on that occasion is remembered. He simply charged Wise [the second of Graves in the Cilley duel) with having entered the House with hands dripping with human blood and a large blotch of gore upon his face, and then presuming to read moral lectures to fellow-members."[22]

Everyone present knew that Wise had been the Kentucky congressman William Graves's second when Graves shot and killed Representative Jonathan Cilley of Maine. The duel, fought on February 24, 1838, had not arisen from longstanding animosity; indeed, it had had little basis save Graves's easily wounded sense of honor. Adams had moved to censure the surviving members of the dueling party, but the motion had not passed. One could argue that compared with what Adams was supposed to have done to merit censure, Wise and Graves were far more culpable. "The prosecution continued, Mr. Adams invariably worsting his opponents; and, finally, several southern members came to his support, and the quarrel was transferred. It now became one at which Mr. Adams and his friends could look and laugh. Southern members were accused of actually contemplating the dissolution of the Union, and one of them of having drawn up resolutions with that design. The final triumph of the Sage of Quincy is well known, and it should teach northern men that lofty courage and honest purpose must always prevail."[23]

Adams's speech in defense of himself took up the better part of six days, beginning on February 2. In it, he reused portions of his oral argument in the *Amistad* case, his earlier statements in and out of the House, and his considerable parliamentary learning. Adams did not occupy the floor alone; some of his remarks were an exchange with Marshall, and some with Wise. The Speaker occasionally had to rule or keep order. Thus the speech was not exactly the kind Adams might have made to a friendly audience out of doors. All during the week, he received death threats through the mails—the evil twin of the antislavery petitions. Although Adams had lost none of his intellectual ability, the speech had a punctuated quality and a plaintive tone, not of surrender but missing the fierceness of his performances in 1836 and 1837. Indeed, his voice was so weakened that it was occasionally inaudible to the *Congressional Globe* reporter of the debates. Although the issue of the gag rule in the House would go on until the closing days of the lame-duck session of the Twenty-Eighth Congress in 1844, Adams's substantive contribution to the debate ended with these remarks.[24]

Adams's speeches on the censure motion have not survived in all their detail. Nor can we return to the chamber and watch as he summoned all his years of learning and experience in the defense of his conduct. According to the *Globe* reporter's summary, "Mr. Adams here went at some length into the history of his past life, his intercourse and friendship with, and the confidence he had enjoyed of Washington, Jefferson, Madison, and Monroe, during their successive presidential terms, as manifest by the various important offices conferred upon him."[25]

Adams by this time was not only a witness to much of the history of the founding of the nation, he was the history of the founding of the nation. In fact, as Adams confided to his diary on more than one occasion, he considered Jefferson a hypocrite and Madison a lightweight. But he was two generations older than his persecutors, and in this period of history both the lionization of the founders and the respect given to old age were on his side. Had Virginia's representatives so fallen from the high station of these founders? The classical theme that an age of gold (the founders') would be followed by ages of lesser metal was one that every educated man knew. Adams was not the first (or the last) to invoke it. "In all his intercourse he had had with these men, from Washington down to Monroe, never, in the course of his life, was there a question [i.e., a disagreement] between them and him on the subject of slavery, He knew that they all abhorred slavery, and he could prove it, if it was denied now, from the testimony of Jefferson, of Madison, and of Washington themselves." While it was true that they had detested slavery, it was also true that they had compromised with it, for all three men had owned many slaves, and had their real wealth been computed, slave property would have made up the bulk of it. The younger Jefferson had had little good to say about slavery (or about African Americans) in his *Notes on the State of Virginia*, and one could find in Madison's and Washington's writings condemnation of the institution. All three men had thought slavery an "evil" but despaired over finding a remedy for it save voluntary emancipation. None of them had been an abolitionist. With Adams vowing to continue his defense for another week, the motion to censure died, 106–93. His closing address to the jury of his peers had been successful.[26]

The end of the gag rule in the House came with a whimper. At the end of the lame-duck session of the Twenty-Seventh Congress, on December 3, 1844, Adams moved that the standing rule be rescinded. Jacob Thompson of Mississippi asked that the motion be tabled, in effect killed, but a 104–81 majority refused. The vote on ending the gag rule then followed, with 108 in favor and 80 opposed. The Democratic Party, long the bastion of the gag rule, voted along sectional lines, with 55 Whigs and 53 Democrats voting aye. Not all of the nay votes came from the South, but only a handful of northerners voted against Adams's motion. At his South Carolina plantation, Silver Bluff, Hammond recorded the event: "The rescinding of the 25 . . . rule of the House at Washington seemed to produce little sensation at [the South Carolina legislative session at] Columbia." A colleague told Hammond that "he was glad it was repealed," for it would allow debate on the issue. Hammond was of a different mind. He had not wanted the issue of slavery debated. "I told him the result of it would be to convert the House of Representatives into an abolition society and to flood our country with incendiary pamphlets."[27]

The Senate version of the gag rule continued until 1850, but it was never as firm as the House's. Its death knell was first sounded on February 7, 1850, when Senator John P. Hale of New Hampshire offered an antislavery petition. It was objected to by southern senators. Hale argued that there was no rule against presenting. He was corrected—there was a usage. Hale wryly responded that southern petitions for slavery were routinely accepted, while his had been rejected. The same exchange for and against annexation of Texas ended with all the petitions referred to committee. After a good deal of tub thumping on both sides, on March 25 William Seward of New York, like Hale an avowed abolitionist, offered a series of antislavery petitions. No objection

The lithograph *Death of John Quincy Adams at the U.S. Capitol Feby. 23d 1848* was a bestseller for the firm of Currier & Ives.

was raised, and the petitions were referred to committee. Like the House rule, the Senate usage had ended with a whimper.[28]

What had changed? Adams had no answer and turned his attention to preventing the annexation of Texas. He failed, but he was accustomed to failure. "The odds are fearful. May God defend the right!" His diary entries for the period do not indicate why he thought he had won, other than that his cause was a righteous one. He rejected once again the notion that he was the head of the antislavery forces in the country. He still conceived his efforts as a defense of constitutional rights rather than of the rights of man, although he had discoursed long and well on the latter in his *Amistad* oral argument.[29]

John Quincy Adams suffered a catastrophic stroke at his desk on the floor of the House. Carried to a room on the Senate side of the Capitol, he lingered for two days. It was his second major attack, the first having kept him from Congress for nearly a year. Attended by friends and former adversaries alike, he died on February 23, 1848.

Historians, as is their wont, have supplied their own answers to the question why the gag rule lost favor in both houses. The rise of the Free-Soil Party, the growing respectability of abolitionism in the North, and the end of slavery in the French and British Empires all surely played a part. A new generation of politicians in the North who were not afraid of the word *abolition* cannot be overlooked. The shifting demography of the nation, with more and more people living north of the Mason-Dixon line, which gave greater weight to northern opinion in the House, contributed to the process. Indeed, this latter development became a threat in itself, as the great spokesman for the gag and for the South would shortly tell the Senate. John C. Calhoun's last great address and a following address by Daniel Webster were the final shots in the long battle over gag rules.

4

"How Can the Union Be Preserved?"

ADAMS HAD WON THE BATTLE BUT, sadly, not the war. His purpose
had shifted over the long and bitter years of debate from opposition to a gag
rule to opposition to slavery. But by the beginning of the 1850s the yoke of
slavery was fixed even more tightly on the necks of the slaves and the politics
of the nation. Southern intellectuals and social leaders no longer apologized
for slavery. Instead, they celebrated it as the highest form of society, a necessary complement to honor, civility, and progress among the master races. As
Edmund Ruffin, a much-respected Virginia agricultural reformer and proslavery publicist, wrote in 1853, "The introduction and establishment of domestic
slavery is necessarily an improvement of the condition and wealth and well
being of the community in general, and also of the comfort of the enslaved
class." Leading southern politicians agreed. As Senator Robert Toombs of
Georgia told a college audience in Oxford, Georgia, "In glancing over the
civilized world, the eye rests upon not a single spot where all classes of society are so well content with their social system, or have greater reason to be
so, than in the slaveholding states of the American Union." That stance made
threats to slavery where it already existed and efforts to prevent its expansion
even more frightening to its defenders.[1]

The demise of the gag rule in the House played a critical role in the next great slavery crisis Congress faced. To be precise, it was the absence of the gag rule that reshaped the public discourse over slavery in the debates over the admission of California to the Union as a free state and the imposition of a new federal fugitive slave law in 1850. A tempest had been brewing for years over the balance of free and slave states in Congress. Despite both Adams's and Van Buren's efforts, Congress and the outgoing president, John Tyler, offered Texas the chance to enter the Union. The incoming president, James K. Polk, urged Texas to accept the terms of the offer, and in 1846 it formally became a state. With the gag rule in place, congressional debates over these matters were perforce limited by the exclusion of abolitionist print literature. With the demise of the gag rule, freedom of speech on the floor of the two houses once again brought the condemnation of slavery front and center and turned a controversy into a crisis.[2]

The annexation of Texas, followed by US claims to a border on the Rio Grande, brought Mexico and the United States to the brink of war. President James K. Polk ordered American troops to patrol the Rio Grande aggressively, and a clash with Mexican forces led to a declaration of war in Congress in 1846. It was a war that slave states wanted and free states dreaded, for all the territory that might come with victory, including the future states of New Mexico, Arizona, and California, might be slave states. Adams opposed the admission of Texas precisely because it would expand the domain of slavery, but a stroke crippled him for much of 1846, and he was unable to attend Congress. If he had been in his seat, he would have applauded David Wilmot, a Pennsylvania Whig, who sought to forestall that event by proposing that no territory acquired from Mexico would be open to slavery. In the House, where free states' population gave them a majority of members, the Wilmot Proviso won. Without a gag rule, the debate focused squarely on the expansion of slavery, Wilmot making clear that his objections to it were based on "viewing slavery as I do." When Adams returned to his seat in the House in 1848, he blasted President Polk for bringing on the war and delaying its conclusion. Meanwhile, in the Senate, led by John C. Calhoun, a majority did not agree to pass the proviso. With the gag rule newly interred in the upper house, he could deplore the proviso and the language accompanying it as an example of "blind fanaticism" and "daringly opposed to the Constitution."[3]

Faced with the threat that the South would secede if the admission of California as a free state were to upset the balance in the Senate, a threat made all too real by the escalating rhetoric in Congress, which a gag rule might have constrained, Senator Henry Clay of Kentucky pulled together a series of compromise bills. Thirty years earlier, Clay had engineered the Missouri Compromise, which included a promise that no territory north of the latitude 36°30' (Missouri's southern boundary) would come into the Union as a slave state. California straddled the line. Its voters had decided that they did not want slavery (or the presence of free persons of color for that matter). Clay proposed that California enter as a free state and that a powerful new federal fugitive slave law accompany its admission. The Fugitive Slave Act of 1850 provided for federal commissioners in the North to aid southern slave catchers. Finally, a bill would have ended the slave trade in the District of Columbia—the objective of the very first antislavery petitions to Congress in 1835.[4]

In response, two of the most famous, perhaps *the* most famous, of all speeches in the Congress came within four days of each other, on March 4 and March 7, 1850. South Carolina's Calhoun delivered the first, Massachusetts's Daniel Webster delivered the second. Both were seemingly about the compromise legislation that Henry Clay had authored. Both men had served in Congress during Adams's tenure there, and both were well acquainted with the gag-rule debates. The frankness with which they confronted the issue was enabled by the end of the gag rule in the Senate. Had there never been a gag rule, these speeches might well have come sooner. Were a gag rule still in place, the two speeches would likely have played differently.

Calhoun, in the last stages of tuberculosis, was carried into the Senate chamber on a couch born by his Virginia colleague James Mason and South Carolina's Andrew Pickens Butler. Mason read Calhoun's speech. It warned of secession if the Congress did not go far enough to protect southern interests. All the previous fall, Calhoun had been sounding the call for secession if more concessions were not made to the South. Note that Calhoun divided the country into North and South, not pro- or antislavery nor Whig versus Democrat. Party divisions, he rightly saw, had been overturned by sectional divisions.[5]

Calhoun could speak with his own personal authority. For much of his political career in the Senate, he had defended the institution of slavery with fierce logic and genuine commitment. He was also a Unionist. "I have, senators, believed from the first that the agitation of the subject of slavery would, if not prevented by some timely and effective measure, end in disunion." His fears of disunion were real enough. Even as he addressed the Senate, "fire-eating" politicians in the South, notably Robert Barnwell Rhett of South Carolina, were agitating for secession. The pressure on the Whig Party in the South was unrelenting and almost unbearable, as politician after politician left his Whig moorings and sailed to the Democratic harbor. "Entertaining this opinion, I have, on all proper occasions, endeavored to call the attention of both the two great parties which divided the country to adopt some measure to prevent so great a disaster, but without success. The agitation has been permitted to proceed with almost no attempt to resist it, until it has reached a point when it can no longer be disguised or denied that the Union is in danger. You have thus had forced upon you the greatest and gravest question that can ever come under your consideration: How can the Union be preserved?"[6]

Calhoun was a master of what might be called classical oratory. (Lincoln was also a master, as was Joshua Giddings. Adams was more a scholarly lecturer than an orator.) Here Calhoun engaged in the rhetorical question, a question to which the interrogator already knows the answer. "To give a satisfactory answer to this mighty question [secession], it is indispensable to have an accurate and thorough knowledge of the nature and the character of the cause by which the Union is endangered. . . . The first question, then, presented for consideration in the investigation I propose to make in order to obtain such knowledge is: What is it that has endangered the Union?"[7]

Though no longer a nationalist, that is, a politician who favored national over state policy initiatives, Calhoun nevertheless loved and honored the Union. His question was not merely rhetorical. He wanted to save the nation to which he had devoted so much of his adult energies. On this occasion, Calhoun was referring to the gag-rule era, beginning with the abolitionist postal campaign. Recall that Calhoun was the author of the Senate version of the gag rule, and it fell into disuse shortly before he died. He did not need to tell the other members of the Senate about it. There was much that followed in his speech that was subtext, that is, it did not need to be explained or expanded. He was addressing a body that had lived through the debates. "To this question there can be but one answer,—that the immediate cause is the almost universal discontent which pervades all the States composing the Southern section of the Union." The cause of the discontent was the prospect of a northern assault on the South's peculiar institution. "This widely extended discontent is not of recent origin. It commenced with the agitation of the slavery question and has been increasing ever since."[8]

Having pinpointed the source of the malady, Calhoun blamed it on the

Photograph of John C. Calhoun, 1849, by Mathew Brady. Emaciated, Calhoun was already dying of tuberculosis. Courtesy of Library of Congress.

acts of certain unthinking politicians. "It is a great mistake to suppose, as is by some, that it originated with demagogues who excited the discontent with the intention of aiding their personal advancement, or with the disappointed ambition of certain politicians who resorted to it as the means of retrieving their fortunes. On the contrary, all the great political influences of the section were arrayed against excitement, and exerted to the utmost to keep the people quiet."[9]

In other words, wise and prudent politicians in Congress (Calhoun foremost among them) had tried to prevent disunion by muzzling the speech of abolitionists and rejecting the petitions abolitionist societies sent to Congress. The means of this wise and prudent policy had been the gag rule. Still, muzzling the petitioners did not muffle the division over slavery so much as make it louder.

Calhoun was a political realist. The question whether a republic so divided by a single interest could survive went all the way back to James Madison's essays in the *Federalist Papers* (1787–88). In defending the Constitution, Madison had argued that the separation of powers among the three branches of the federal government and the retention of state sovereignty alongside the sovereignty of the national government ensured that no single interest or section could gain control of the whole and thus impose its particular point of view on the rest of the country. But for Madison, the only guarantee that these safeguards would work had been the existence of a national union. In the march to the dissolution of the Union, the abolitionists decried the slave interest as one such tyranny, and Calhoun saw the free-soil movement as such a tyranny, at least potentially.[10]

Calhoun's realism was as much economic as it was political. He was a devotee of practical, statistical theories. In 1836, after reading the work of Francis Lieber, a Prussian legalist teaching at the college in Columbia, South Carolina, Calhoun treated the Senate to a plea for more complete analysis of the American economy. Behind the call for better information was, no doubt, Calhoun's belief that American economic progress rested on the export of southern staples. As it happened, there was much truth to that lower-level causal thesis. Its political application would come in the Senate from Calhoun's successor, the very same James Henry Hammond, when he told the upper house that slavery and cotton would make the South the center of an American empire, for "in this territory lies the great valley of the Mississippi, now the real, and soon to be the acknowledged seat of the empire of the world. The sway of that valley will be as great as ever the Nile knew in the earlier ages of mankind. We own the most of it. The most valuable part of it belongs to us now; and although those who have settled above us are now opposed to us, another generation will tell a different tale. They are ours by all the laws of nature; slave-labor will go over every foot of this great valley where it will be found profitable to use it, and some of those who may not use it are soon to be united with us by such ties as will make us one and inseparable."[11]

Calhoun was not so sanguine as Hammond. He saw danger where Hammond would see opportunity, for the upper reaches of the Mississippi lay in the Midwest, the home of much of the "long-continued agitation of the slave question on the part of the North, and the many aggressions which they have made on the rights of the South." The result was that "the equilibrium between the two sections in the government as it stood when the Constitution was ratified and the government put in action has been destroyed." For Calhoun had seen the growth of the free-soil territories, expanding to the

West, and the slave territories confined, imprisoned in the existing lands of the South. Slavery so confined would consume itself, and the section with it. "The result of the whole is to give the Northern section a predominance in every department of the government, and thereby concentrate in it the two elements which constitute the federal government: a majority of States, and a majority of their population, estimated in federal numbers. Whatever section concentrates the two in itself possesses the control of the entire government." It was simply a matter of statistics—of numbers, space, and wealth.

Thus, even if Madison had been right about the safety of a Union in the founding era, for Calhoun Madison's arguments for the value of union disappeared when one section dominated the federal government. The shift from interests and parties (in Madison's terminology) to sections (Calhoun's word) was an ominous one, for sectional division was geographical, and there was no way to change geography, as there might have been for Whig and Democratic party alignments. In short, if one followed Calhoun in this shift of terms, there was no basis for compromise; the two sections were already different nations.[12]

Calhoun watched with mounting concern as immense numbers of German and Irish immigrants, along with numbers of Scandinavians, went North, not South (in part because the immigrants did not want to compete with slaves and in part because they did not like the idea of human bondage). In terms of states added to the Union and population (the basis for representation in the Senate and the House, respectively), the southern states would increasingly be in the minority. Worse, as slavery concentrated in the South, the numbers of slaves and the danger they posed to their masters would grow. For the slave system to be safe, slavery had to be dispersed. "Had this destruction [of the equality of the sections] been the operation of time without the interference of government," said Calhoun, "the South would have had no reason to complain; but such was not the fact. It was caused by the legislation of this government, which was appointed as the common agent of all and charged with the protection of the interests and security of all." Calhoun then offered a brief and somewhat tilted version of the history of the political party system. "The great mass of the people of the South were divided, as in the other section, into Whigs and Democrats. The leaders and the presses of both parties in the South were very solicitous to prevent excitement and to preserve quiet; because it was seen that the effects of the former would necessarily tend to weaken, if not destroy, the political ties which united them with their respective parties in the other section." To this extent he was correct: so long as both Whigs and Democrats were national parties, and so long as the leaders of both were determined to minimize or avoid the slavery issue, disunion was not in prospect. "But, great as it was, it was not sufficient to prevent the widespread discontent which now pervades the section."[13]

Calhoun understood how the party leaders of his era had used the changing rules for voting (e.g., getting rid of property qualifications for voters) to build the Jacksonian Democratic Party. As his own ambitions for the presidency faded in the 1820s, he became more and more convinced that a government based on the will of the common man, that is, a democracy, was dangerous to property rights. This view should have put him in the Whig Party, alongside Henry Clay and Daniel Webster, but in the end, Calhoun, like Adams, was a man largely above political parties, in that simple allegiance to a political party meant less to him than allegiance to a cause—the defense of the white southern way of life.

Calhoun here reached the core of his argument: how the sections differed over slavery. He might simply have begun his address at this point, saying that slavery would never be safe in a union dominated by free-soil or, worse, abolitionist thinking. Even here, he did not open with slavery as an economic system, as Hammond had. Instead, he portrayed it as a social system, a set of relations between two races. He had said all this before, in defense of the gag rule in the Senate. Then he had spoken with assurance; now his words, read by another, sounded hollow and desperate, for the gag rule had not done its job.

Every portion of the North entertains views and feelings more or less hostile to [slavery]. Those most opposed and hostile regard it as a sin, and consider themselves under the most sacred obligation to use every effort to destroy it. Indeed, to the extent that they conceive that they have power, they regard themselves as implicated in the sin, and responsible for not suppressing it by the use of all and every means. Those less opposed and hostile regard it as a crime—an offense against humanity, as they call it and, altho not so fanatical, feel themselves bound to use all efforts to effect the same object; while those who are least opposed and hostile regard it as a blot and a stain on the character of what they call the "nation," and feel themselves accordingly bound to give it no countenance or support. On the contrary, the Southern section regards the relation as one which cannot be destroyed without subjecting the two races to the greatest calamity, and the section to poverty, desolation, and wretchedness; and accordingly they feel bound by every consideration of interest and safety to defend it.[14]

Calhoun saw the final outcome as occurring not within weeks or months but eventually. "Unless something decisive is done, I again ask, What is to stop this agitation before the great and final object at which it aims—the abolition of slavery in the States—is consummated? Is it, then, not certain that if something is not done to arrest it, the South will be forced to choose between abolition and secession? Indeed, as events are now moving, it will not require the South to secede in order to dissolve the Union. Agitation will of itself effect it, of which its past history furnishes abundant proof." Calhoun had seen how the movement against slavery had gone from a relative handful of reformers seeking to persuade southerners to give up slavery to a national political movement. He did not differentiate between the Free-Soilers, who simply did not want slavery to expand into new territories, and the abolitionists, who wanted to end slavery where it already existed. Perhaps in his mind the two were synonymous, or perhaps he thought the free-soil movement would eventually become abolitionism. In fact, the free-soil movement was folded into the new Republican Party in 1856, but that party's platform never endorsed the forcible freeing of slaves in the slave states. It was fear for the future, rather than current political realities, that drove Calhoun's thinking on this point.[15]

Calhoun was dying. He knew it, his fellow senators knew it, his friends and family in South Carolina knew it. Deathbed sentiments were a fixture of nineteenth-century Victorian literature. In poetry, eulogy, and the novel a central figure's last words had heightened meaning. A good death brought closure to a good life. Calhoun's couch was not his deathbed (he died at home, on March 31), but his last speech in the Senate was a kind of deathbed scene, full of pathos. Would the Union survive, or would it, like Calhoun, die? "It is a great mistake to suppose that disunion can be effected by a single blow. The cords which bind these States together in one common Union are far too numerous and powerful for that. Disunion must be the work of time. It is only through a long process, and successively, that the cords can be snapped until the whole fabric falls asunder."[16]

Calhoun had reached the peroration, the concluding portion of his address. Every ear must have been strained to the utmost to hear what Calhoun had written. He was a great man, as great as Adams, though his ambition for the highest office had never been fulfilled. This was his final hour, and his address lived up to it. "If the agitation goes on, the same force, acting with increased intensity, as has been shown, will finally snap every cord, when nothing will be left to hold the States together except force." Surely there was another way. "How can the Union be saved? To this I answer, there is but one way by which it can be, and that is by adopting such measures as will satisfy the States belonging to the Southern section that they can remain in the Union consistently with their honor and their safety." Calhoun was a lawyer, and ultimately the solution must be found in law rather than in partisanship. "There is but one way by which it can with any certainty; and that is by a full and final settlement, on the principle of justice, of all the questions at issue between the two sections. The South asks for justice, simple justice, and less she ought not to take. She has no compromise to offer but the Constitution, and no concession or surrender to make. She has already surrendered so much that she has little left to surrender." Legislation protecting slave property was the answer. "There will be no difficulty in devising such a provision—one that will protect the South, and which at the same time will improve and strengthen the government instead of impairing and weakening it. But will the North agree to this? It is for her to answer the question. But, I will say, she cannot refuse if she has half the love of the Union which she professes to have, or without justly exposing herself to the charge that her love of power and aggrandizement is far greater than her love of the Union." Calhoun was pleading with free-state senators to accept a comprehensive and binding fugitive slave law, little realizing, or perhaps fully realizing but refusing to credit, that such a law would become only another irritant between free and slave states.[17]

One can only imagine how John Quincy Adams, dead two years by that time, might have replied to Calhoun. Instead a reply came from another Massachusetts man, Senator Daniel Webster. It was not quite a concession to all Calhoun's demands, for Calhoun opposed the compromise proposals and Webster embraced them. But it was hardly what antislavery advocates wanted to hear. If Calhoun looked backwards to a republic of honor and deference, Webster looked forward to a nation of eager entrepreneurs. Calhoun held himself (when ambition did not dictate otherwise) to the ideal of a planter-gentleman. His substantial plantation, Fort Hill, was not the wealthiest in upland South Carolina, but Calhoun had married well and lived well. Webster had come from dirt farmers in New Hampshire and worked his way up from a law practice in Portsmouth to leadership of the Boston Bar. There Webster was known as a dogged advocate of New England commercial and later industrial interests. If Adams represented the old puritan strain in New England culture, Webster represented the commercial and industrial elements in New England. Adams rarely lawyered for lucre. Webster was a high-priced counsel who had taken retainers from the Bank of the United States and other corporate entities. Adams was a lawyer in the highest sense of the term, a spokesman for the higher law. Webster was a hireling for the best-paying client. On this occasion Webster tried to step up to Adams's pedestal, putting aside local and monetary interests in the name of a higher good. But he could not restrain his penchant for embellishment, which over the next three hours ran rampant.[18]

Webster had always been regarded as antislavery, if not rabidly abolitionist. He had introduced antislavery petitions in the Senate during its March 1836 sessions. He had opposed the annexation of Texas and any expansion of slavery. Now, however, he begged the Senate to choose union over equality. Webster was one of the greatest orators of the age, a first choice for Fourth of July and other ceremonial occasions. His speech in the Senate on the compromise proposals was much anticipated.[19]

Webster was among a group of Massachusetts public figures who were always in demand as public speakers. While some of their performances comprised only general and often-repeated bromides, on this occasion Webster departed from the content of his previous addresses. The result must have been a collective intake of breath among his colleagues. His first theme was the deliberative nature of the upper house, a place not given to rushed or harsh judgements. "I wish to speak to-day, not as a Massachusetts man, nor as a Northern man, but as an American, and a member of the Senate of the United States." Webster was not above pandering to the self-importance of his colleagues, but his reflection is somewhat reminiscent of a farewell address: "It is fortunate that there is a Senate of the United States; a body not yet moved from its propriety, not lost to a just sense of its own dignity and its own high responsibilities, and a body to which the country looks, with confidence, for wise, moderate, patriotic, and healing counsels. It is not to be denied that we live in the midst of strong agitations, and are surrounded by very considerable dangers to our institutions and our government."[20]

Daniel Webster, ca. 1847. The Roman brow and the deep-set eyes were then regarded as qualities of intellect as well as physical appearance. Courtesy of Library of Congress.

Webster's very first passages should have alerted his audience to the shift in his stance. He now called for moderation in the face of agitation. Perhaps he had withered into the truth? His longstanding ambition for the presidency had not quite dimmed, and he, along with Clay, had come to value the Union as if it were their creation rather than their forebears'. Certainly the speech that followed strove for a higher tone than mere partisanship would allow. Some historians have found a consistent thread in Webster's attachment to New England business interests and his new concessions to the South. New England merchants and bankers had a good deal invested in southern cotton production. New England textiles and shoes clothed and shod the slaves.[21]

Whatever his motives might be, those in the galleries and the members listened intently to the torrent of words, the cascading images, a pattern of public speaking mastered by this exemplar of all New England's orators. Delivered in a solemn tone, forcefully, still carrying something of the twang of the Boston he had made his home for so many years, Webster hammered his points home. Not really a gentleman, certainly not elegant or even attractive in appearance, Webster had eyes that compelled attention. Black as anthracite coal, they were the reason for the nickname Black Dan:

> The imprisoned winds are let loose. The East, the North, and the stormy South combine to throw the whole sea into commotion, to toss its billows to the skies, and disclose its profoundest depths. I do not affect to regard myself . . . as holding, or as fit to hold, the helm in this combat with the political elements; but I have a duty to perform, and I mean to perform it with fidelity, not without a sense of existing dangers, but not without hope. I have a part to act, not for my own security or safety, for I am looking out for no fragment upon which to float away from the wreck, if wreck there must be, but for the good of the whole, and the preservation of all.[22]

Although Webster's tenure as secretary of state in the Tyler administration included many achievements, among them a treaty with Great Britain defining the boundary of the United States and Canada that still stands, his reputation rested on his skills as an advocate rather than as a statesman. Now his client was the Union, as Adams's had been the Constitution and Calhoun's the South. Could he persuade the jury—his fellow senators—to accept the compromise that Clay had fashioned?

> I speak to-day for the preservation of the Union. . . . I speak to-day, out of a solicitous and anxious heart for the restoration to the country of that quiet and harmonious harmony which make the blessings of this Union so rich, and so dear to us all. These are the topics I propose to myself to discuss; these are the motives, and the sole motives, that influence me in the wish to communicate my opinions to the Senate and the country; and if I can do anything, however little, for the promotion of these ends, I shall have accomplished all that I expect.[23]

So much for proof of Webster's good intentions; now to the question of the day, slavery. Note that like Calhoun, Webster saw slavery as a sectional issue between a free North and a slave South. In fact this was not true. Many areas of the Upper South, for example, eastern Tennessee and eastern Kentucky, and even parts of the Deep South, for example, northeastern Georgia, northeastern Alabama, and western North Carolina, had few slaves. These areas of the South were populated with white family farmers. In parts of the North slavery was still fastened on some men and women, for example, in New Jersey. Harsh "black codes" in Illinois and the influence of slave owners in Ohio and Indiana denied free blacks rights that their fellow citizens enjoyed. But so powerful was the geographical image of free North and slave South that Webster unthinkingly adopted it.

> Now, Sir, upon the general nature and influence of slavery there exists a wide difference of opinion between the northern portion of this country and the southern. It is said on the one side, that . . . slavery is a wrong; that it is founded merely in the right of the strongest; and that is an oppression. . . . These are the sentiments that are cherished, and of late with greatly augmented force, among the people of the Northern States. They have taken hold of the religious sentiment of that part of the country, as they have, more or less, taken hold of the religious feeling of a considerable portion of mankind. The South, upon the other side, having been accustomed to this relation between two races all their lives, from their birth, having been taught, in general, to treat the subjects of this bondage with care and kindness, and I believe, in general, feeling great kindness for them, have not taken the view of the subject which I have mentioned. There are thousands of religious men, with consciences as tender as any of their brethren at the North, who do not see the unlawfulness of slavery.[24]

Webster was aware that the antebellum period was one of great religiosity. The Second Great Awakening had swept through the country, with well-attended churches and mass revival meetings on campgrounds. At first, Methodist and Baptist ministers, moving South, had opposed slavery, but by 1850 a second generation of southern ministers had become some of its most consistent and vociferous defenders, asking only that masters treat their slaves with kindness and slaves accept their subordination with good grace.[25]

A shared religiosity was one of the bonds Calhoun cited as holding the nation together. In truth, conferences and associations of Baptists, Episcopalians, and Methodists spanned the nation. But over the period of the gag-rule debates, northern congregations began to oppose slavery at the same time that southern congregations proclaimed slavery a positive good. National church organizations split along sectional lines. Slavery thus cut the ties of religious affiliation that had held the nation together, becoming the grounds for the "recrimination" that Webster decried.[26]

Webster had been at the center of antebellum politics long enough to know how dangerous it was to blame parties and partisans for what was a far deeper rift. "In the excited times in which we live, there is found to exist a state of crimination and recrimination between the North and South. There are lists of grievances produced by each; and those grievances, real or supposed, alienate the minds of one portion of the country from the other, exasperate the feelings, and subdue the sense of fraternal affection, patriotic love, and mutual regard." Slavery was the worm in the bud. By 1850 little of the fraternal affection remained. One must remember that Webster was a lawyer with a huge and highly remunerative practice. He saw the world not in moral terms but in legal ones. "In particular, the free states' people's unwillingness to assist slave catchers . . . a disinclination to perform fully their constitutional duties in regard to the return of persons bound to service who have escaped into the free States" was just grounds for southern complaints in Webster's opinion.[27]

In context, Webster was defending the proposed fugitive slave bill. It imposed an expense on the nation in more ways than one by creating a federal bureaucracy to ensure that runaway slaves were recaptured and returned to the South. That southern states'-rights advocates gathered behind a major extension of national power, while northern opponents of states' rights embraced that concept to argue against the proposed law was one of the many ironies of the age. For in response to the first slave "rendition" act, in 1793, some northern states passed personal-liberty laws. These gave to persons of color snatched by professional slave catchers the rights of any other citizen of the free states, including the right to have their status adjudicated in a court of law by a jury. Webster also knew that antislavery demonstrators in northern states had attempted to free slaves held in jail for their masters.[28]

Like Calhoun, Webster assayed a legal solution to what he saw as a legal problem. Laws must be obeyed, whatever one's personal opinion might be. "Every member of every Northern legislature is bound by oath, like every other officer in the country, to support the Constitution of the United States; and the article of the Constitution which says to these States that they shall deliver up fugitives from service is as binding in honor and conscience as any other article." In language that easily could have applied to Adams, Webster reminded the members that "no man fulfills his duty in any legislature who sets himself to find excuses, evasions, escapes from this constitutional obligation." But Webster was careful not to blame any of the national legislators. "I have always thought that the Constitution addressed itself to the legislatures of the States or to the States themselves . . . and I confess I have always been of the opinion that it was an injunction upon the States themselves."[29]

Some states, like Pennsylvania, passed antikidnapping laws that criminalized catching and carrying off supposed slaves without first bringing them before a state judge. The Pennsylvania law was found unconstitutional by the Supreme Court in *Prigg v. Pennsylvania* (1842), but that same decision by the Massachusetts justice Joseph Story found that state officials could not be required to aid and abet the slave catchers. It was a federal matter. The decision split the high court, with southern justices like Roger Taney and Peter Daniel insisting that the Fugitive Slave Act of 1793 required state officials to aid in the rendition of runaways.[30]

Webster found refuge in a strict legalism that allowed him to exclude any reference to the evils of slavery. "My habit is to respect the result of judicial deliberations and the solemnity of judicial decisions." If the free states would not assist in the recapture and return of runaway slaves, "the business of seeing that these fugitives are delivered up resides in the power of Congress and the national judicature." He joined Calhoun in the call for a new federal law in which federal officials called "commissioners" would aid federal marshals and federal courts in rendering to the South what it desired: complete control over its slave laborers even when they were no longer in slave lands. "What right have [state authorities] in their legislative capacity or any other capacity, to endeavor to get round this Constitution, or to embarrass the free exercise of the rights secured by the Constitution to the persons whose slaves escape from them? None at all." There was no doubt of the constitutionality of a fugitive slave law. Article 4, section 2, clause 3, of the Constitution provided that "no person held to service or labour in one state, under the laws thereof, escaping into another, shall, in consequence of any law or regulation therein, be discharged from such service or labour, but shall be delivered up on claim of the party to whom such service or labour may be due." The problem came in determining who such persons might be. The answer of the fugitive slave bill of 1850 was to penalize anyone who helped such suspected slaves escape from recapture or rendition, but the underlying problem remained: who was to determine whether an individual was a runaway of a free person of color, and how was that determination to be made? To assume, as the law did, that any person of color living or passing through a free state was such a runaway made slavery national rather than sectional.[31]

Webster could not ignore the gag-rule era. It dominated all debate in Congress for nearly a decade and a half. But he could offer an apology to southern members of Congress for the gag rule being gone. One way to do this was to excoriate the abolitionists who had launched the petition campaign. At the same time, he could not, and would not, offend his many Massachusetts constituents who had joined their ranks. "Then, Sir, there are the Abolition societies, of which I am unwilling to speak." There followed a Ciceronian outburst. (Cicero, a famous Roman orator, politician, and lawyer, often said that he would not touch a subject, then went on about it for hours.) "But in regard to [abolitionist societies] I have very clear notions and opinions. I do not think them useful. I think their operations for the last twenty years have produced nothing good or valuable. At the same time, I believe thousands of their members to be honest and good men, perfectly well-meaning men." This was faint praise, oddly reminiscent of Adams's own views at the outset of the gag-rule controversy. The abolitionists "have excited feelings; they think they must do something for the cause of liberty; and, in their sphere of action, they do not see what else they can do than to contribute to an Abolition press, or an Abolition society, or to pay an Abolition lecturer."[32]

The "heckler's veto" is a logical error. When hecklers are able to shout down a speaker or disrupt a meeting and then turn around and claim that the speech or the meeting led to disorder, they are engaging in the hecklers' veto. When southern mobs illegally seized and destroyed federal mails and threatened abolitionist speakers, or southern members of Congress shouted down Adams and then turned around and blamed him for causing disorder in the House, they were engaging in the hecklers' veto on a grand scale. Webster's broad hint that the abolitionists' activities had been responsible for the misconduct of mobs and led to even more stringent versions of slave law embraced the illogic of the hecklers' veto. Webster had in mind the abolitionists' postal campaign, the antislavery petitions, and the gag-rule debates when he continued, "As has been said by the honorable member from South Carolina [Calhoun], these Abolition societies commenced their course of action in 1835. It is said, I do not know how true it may be, that they sent incendiary publications into the slave States; at any rate, they attempted to arouse, and did arouse, a very strong feeling; in other words, they created great agitation in the North against Southern slavery. Well, what was the result? The bonds of the slave were bound more firmly than before, their rivets were more strongly fastened."[33]

In 1832, after the suppression of Nat Turner's slave rebellion, the legislature of the state of Virginia seriously considered a gradual ending of slavery in the state. It is true that some members of the legislature, shaken by the re-bellion's proof that not all slaves loved their masters, wanted slaves removed from the state, but in a sense this was nothing new. Slave owners in Virginia had long practiced selling off recalcitrant slaves to planters in the West Indies. In the antebellum era, Virginia was a giant nursery of slaves, supplying them to the cotton plantations along the Mississippi River. Moreover, to imply, as Webster did, that abolitionism of the late 1830s was responsible for Virginia's decision to retain its slaves in 1831 is another example of logical fallacy.[34]

Webster had often held the floor of the Senate for hours with long dis-courses on subjects of interest to his commercial and industrial constituents. This time he tried to portray himself as the representative of a nation, not a state. "Mr. President, I should much prefer to have heard from every member on this floor declarations of opinion that this Union could never be dissolved, than the declaration of opinion by anybody, that, in any case, under the pres-sure of any circumstances, such a dissolution was possible." He was genuinely distressed to hear the word *secession*. "Secession! . . . Peaceable secession. The dismemberment of this vast country without convulsion! The breaking up of the fountains of the great deep without ruffling the surface! Who is so foolish, I beg every body's pardon, as to expect to see any such thing?"[35]

In 1861, many leading southern politicians assumed that the Union could be dissolved without bloodshed. True, there were many in the South who wished to test their manhood in what they later called the "War of Northern Aggression." They flocked to the Confederate colors. In the North, maintain-ing the Union became a patriotic cause, and northern farm boys and city workers enlisted in the Union army. For these men, the prospect of war was a test of manliness and patriotic fervor. As the former Confederate senior com-mander James Longstreet wrote in his memoir of the war, "I believe there is to-day, *because of the war*, a broader and deeper patriotism in all Americans." For Webster to see in 1850 that disunion would bring civil war was testimony to his insight into the psyche of the nation. "Peaceable secession is an utter impossibility. Is the great Constitution under which we live, covering this whole country, is it to be thawed and melted away by secession, as the snows on the mountain melt under the influence of a vernal sun, disappear almost unobserved, and run off?" There would be no peace. "Sir, I see as plainly as I see the sun in heaven what that disruption itself must produce; I see that it must produce war," a war so terrible that even Webster's store of metaphors could not describe the carnage. Webster had never seen or participated in combat, but his vision of a civil war was very close to what would occur when secession came.[36]

Perhaps because he could recall the kind of patriotism that the Mexican-American War had engendered in the South and the antipathy to the war in the North, Webster drew back to the safer ground of legalistic questions. Here he spoke as a lawyer, following the conventions of courtroom discourse. He raised questions, then answered them in a way that bolstered his case. "Why, what would be the result? Where is the line to be drawn? What States are to secede? What is to remain American? What am I . . . An American no longer? Am I to become a sectional man, a local man, a separatist, with no country in common with the gentlemen who sit around me here, or who fill the other house of Congress?" Would one side pay "alimony" to the other? To these he added patriotic images retained from his many Fourth of July speeches. "Where is the flag of the republic to remain? Where is the eagle still to tower? or is he to cower, and shrink, and fall to the ground? Why, Sir, our ancestors, our fathers and our grandfathers, those of them that are yet living amongst us with prolonged lives, would rebuke and reproach us; and our children and our grandchildren would cry out shame upon us." Webster likened the Union to a wedding. But the marriage of the states was teetering on divorce. Domestic bliss, the ideal of marriage in this age of sentiment, had given way to domestic discord. In the 1850s the legal nature of marriage and divorce was in a state of flux. Divorce was still uncommon, but infamous divorce cases shared the pages of newspapers with accounts of national politics. Webster's use of the metaphor borrowed from private law to make a striking point about public law.[37]

If the marital analogy was a little farfetched, an appeal to patriotism was very common. A shared history, culture, language, and tradition was one of the bonds that Calhoun had supposed held the nation together. In the years after the War of 1812, historical societies and fraternal organizations grew up around patriotism. Webster, in sounding the alarm, was inverting the symbols and shared understandings of patriotism. The eagle would cower instead of spread its wings and leave a great nation prey to petty divisions. Such fears were not new. As Calhoun had written to Andrew Jackson on June 1, 1820, in the midst of the controversy over Missouri statehood, "I perceive you have strong foreboding as to our future policy. The discussion on the Missouri question has undoubtedly contributed to weaken in some degree the attachment of our southern and western people to the Union."[38]

Webster knew that Calhoun, among others, had broached the subject of a confederacy of southern states. Calhoun had implied that this was a last resort. Others in Congress, notably Robert Barnwell Rhett of South Carolina, found the prospect of a southern confederacy more attractive. As Rhett opined shortly after the Compromise of 1850 became law, "There will be no fight, but when our southern confederacy is formed, it will not be long before these northern men will crawl to us and beg to be admitted into our union." In the face of such provocative language what was Webster to say?

> I am sorry, Sir, that [secession] has ever been thought of, talked of, or dreamed of, in the wildest flights of human imagination. But the idea, so far as it exists, must be of a separation, assigning the slave States to one side and the free States to the other. Sir, I may express myself too strongly, perhaps, but there are impossibilities in the natural as well as in the physical world, and I hold the idea of a separation of these States, those that are free to form one government, and those that are slave-holding to form another, as such an impossibility. We could not separate the States by any such line, if we were to draw it. We could not sit down here to-day and draw a line of separation that would satisfy any five men in the country. There are natural causes that would keep and tie us together, and there are social and domestic relations which we could not break if we would, and which we should not if we could.[39]

Why deny the coming storm? Webster had lived by the word. As a lawyer, he won by argument, sometimes standing in front of the Supreme Court and speaking for hours on end. As a politician he was without parallel as an orator; in debate no one could best him. Perhaps, just perhaps, once more words would avail him. Surely he believed that the cause of the Union demanded his very best oratorical effort, and he had been working on the speech for many days.

Webster understood the importance of the Mississippi as an internal highway, carrying the produce of the Midwest to the Gulf of Mexico, and thence to the world. "Sir, nobody can look over the face of this country at the present moment, nobody can see where its population is the most dense and growing, without being ready to admit, and compelled to admit, that ere long the strength of America will be in the Valley of the Mississippi. Well, now, Sir, I beg to inquire what the wildest enthusiast has to say about the possibility of cutting that river in two, and leaving free States at its source and on its branches, and slave States down near its mouth, each forming a separate government?" The prospect of having the mouth of the Mississippi in foreign hands had led Jefferson to agree to the Louisiana Purchase. Perhaps the importance of New Orleans to the cotton and sugar trade of the South outweighed its importance to the North, but Mississippi basin's cotton and sugar wealth was shared by northern banking and commercial interests. Surely it would be economic suicide for the river to be cut across a north-south line? A very great public speaker was the master of the peroration, the final passages of a speech designed to inspire and uplift the audience. Webster's peroration was a masterwork.

> And now, Mr. President, instead of speaking of the possibility or utility of secession, instead of dwelling in those caverns of darkness, instead of groping with those ideas so full of all that is horrid and horrible, let us come out into the light of day; let us enjoy the fresh air of Liberty and Union; let us cherish those hopes which belong to us; let us devote ourselves to those great objects that are fit for our consideration and action; let us raise our conceptions to the magnitude and the importance of the duties that devolve upon us; let our comprehension be as broad as the country for which we act, our asperations as high as its certain destiny; let us not be pigmies in a case that calls for men.

Marrying manliness, a private virtue, to great (public) objects was Webster's attempt to resuscitate the founders' goal of disinterested republican civic virtue. This was the ideal of public service as the highest good. Politics in the middle period had sacrificed civic virtue, he feared, in favor of private gain. Thus he called on his listeners to return to the ideals of the founders.

> Never did there devolve on any generation of men higher trusts than now devolve upon us, for the preservation of this Constitution and the harmony and peace of all who are destined to live under it. Let us make our generation one of the strongest and brightest links in that golden chain which is destined, I fondly believe, to grapple the people of all the States to this Constitution for ages to come. We have a great, popular, constitutional government, guarded by law and by judicature, and defended by

the affections of the whole people. No monarchical throne presses these States together, no iron chain of military power encircles them; they live and stand under a government popular in its form, representative in its character, founded upon principles of equality, and so constructed, we hope, as to last forever. In all its history it has been beneficent; it has trodden down no man's liberty; it has crushed no State. Its daily respiration is liberty and patriotism; its yet youthful veins are full of enterprise, courage, and honorable love of glory and renown. Large before, the country has now, by recent events, become vastly larger. This republic now extends, with a vast breadth, across the whole continent. The two great seas of the world wash the one and the other shore.[40]

Webster's speech was carried in all the major newspapers. Some praised him. Others called him a turncoat. No one could deny that the nation had watched and listened. In a way it was the end of an era, for Webster, Clay, and Calhoun would shortly join John Quincy Adams in final repose. In a way it was also the end of an era of great congressional orations, perhaps a fitting close to the story that began with the gag rule. No one gagged the next generation of legislators, but no one rivaled the orators of the gag-rule era. For a time, the Union was intact. For all the politicians' fears that a full discussion of slavery in the Congress would lead to secession, abolitionist petitions did not lead to slave rebellion. When in 1859 an abolitionist named John Brown tried to lead a slave rebellion, not only did he fail but no slaves rallied to his cause. Not only was the Union intact but slavery in the South was undisturbed. For the abolitionists of the North and the slave power of the South, it seemed as if the gag-rule debates had never happened. But appearances in this case were deceptive.[41]

"The Righteousness of Such a War as This Is"

THERE ARE MANY IFS ASSOCIATED with the gag-rule debates. If Adams had not led the fight against the gag rule and in winning the fight proved that the North could rally around an antislavery position, would the southern members of Congress have become so fearful of their northern colleagues that they preferred the risks of secession and civil war to the status quo? If the gag-rule debates had not taken place or at least had not gone on for so long, generating such increasingly fierce rhetoric, would the party system have fractured and been replaced by a sectional system? If Congress had not rehearsed the themes and variations of gag rules, would the Compromise of 1850, the Kansas-Nebraska Act of 1854, and Bleeding Kansas have happened at all? Had Adams not won the battle to allow the word *abolition* into the chambers of Congress, would abolitionists like Theodore Dwight Weld have looked at the carnage of the Civil War and approved "the righteousness of such a war as this"? There are too many ifs.[1]

Historians are wary of dealing with ifs. The fact is that the gag-rule debates played a part in the shift in Congress from party allegiance to sectional allegiance. Were they a cause of the growing chasm between the sections? Yes.

Were they the sole cause? No. But the irony of the gag-rule story should not be lost on anyone. A parliamentary maneuver meant to still a quarrel became an incentive to quarrel, and a rule meant to keep order in the chambers became an incitement to uproar in the chambers. As Adams wrote in his diary on December 13, 1838, he could not doubt "that the fall of slavery is predetermined. But the conflict will be terrible."[2]

More charitably to the participants, one might regard the gag-order resolutions as compromise measures, much like the Missouri Compromise, which preceded them, and the Compromise of 1850, which marked the end of gagging. Seen in this light, the collapse of bipartisan support for the gag rule sent a much less hopeful message than Adams thought. It showed that compromise was increasingly difficult. The members simply gave up trying to mute the slavery controversy. Instead, they embraced it with renewed vigor. By the end of the antebellum era, almost every politician could see what Senator William Seward of New York told an audience in 1858:

> It is an irrepressible conflict between opposing and enduring forces, and it means that the United States must and will, sooner or later, become either entirely a slave-holding nation or entirely a free-labor nation. Either the cotton and rice-fields of South Carolina and the sugar plantations of Louisiana will ultimately be tilled by free labor, and Charleston and New Orleans become marts for legitimate merchandise alone, or else the rye-fields and wheat-fields of Massachusetts and New York must again be surrendered by their farmers to slave culture and to the production of slaves, and Boston and New York become once more markets for trade in the bodies and souls of men.

Even if the crisis of the Union was not as inevitable as Seward seemed to imply, the failure of compromises like the gag order showed how fragile the very notion of compromise had become.[3]

Defenders of the gag at first made moderation the centerpiece of their arguments. They sought a consensus that manumission was best left to the masters and slave law best left to the states. Over time, and battered by the rhetoric of the petitions' presenters, defenders of the gag rule pushed this theme to the side and replaced it with a defense of the South and its institutions. Opponents of the gag rule had at first only wanted the antislavery petitions referred to committee. Harried by the gag-rule proponents, men like Adams began to strike at slavery itself. Again, the internal logic of the arguments had pushed the members beyond their original positions into new and far more divisive stances.

In this sense, it was not politicians' ambition or ineptitude but the intractability of the slavery issue itself that brought on a civil war. The gag-rule debates were a proxy for the debate over slavery. They omened more divisive and overt debates during the 1846–48 war with Mexico. The Wilmot Proviso debates in 1846 over slavery in territories won in the war against Mexico revealed a free North standing more or less united against a slave South. The Compromise of 1850 won a respite that the Kansas-Nebraska Act debates ended in 1854. The two great national parties divided along sectional lines—free soil or the expansion of slavery. What presidential nominee James Buchanan would lament in 1856 as "geographical parties" divided the nation between the new Republican Party and the democracy. No effusion of words in petitions or in congressional debates would settle the slavery question. The defeat of the gag rule in the House was even cited by South Carolina secessionists as one more proof that the North as a whole inflicted on the South "abolitionist petitions, intended to annoy and insult us." Four years of civil war were required to reach that end. The house was dividing against itself, as another great orator (who opposed the war) would soon explain.[4]

In a final echo of the gag-rule debates, the abolitionists once more opened a petition campaign in 1862, this time to convince the wartime Congress and President Abraham Lincoln to end slavery. Petitions arrived in Washington daily, the renewed postal campaign organized by some of the same abolitionists who had played a role in the gag-rule debates. Lincoln, unlike Jackson, Buchanan, and Polk, was inclined to listen, as did Republican antislavery members of Congress. With the members from the secessionist states gone, the debate over slavery had an entirely different cast. Abolitionism was abroad in both chambers. Even Democrats who opposed the universal emancipation of slaves no longer defended slavery as a positive good. Abolitionists in and out of Congress could at last glimpse a time when freedom would be the hallmark of the nation. The object of the first abolitionist crusade, the ending of slavery in the District of Columbia, came to pass in 1862. Congress would draft and submit to the states an amendment to the Constitution ending slavery in 1865. By that time, Adams's prediction that the conflict against the slave power would be "terrible" had come to pass. But that is another story.[5]

NOTES

Prologue

1. *Congressional Globe*, 21st Cong., 1st sess., 79–81 (1835). On the vote in the Virginia House of Delegates four years earlier, see Alfred L. Brophy, *University, Court, and Slave: Pro-Slavery Thought in Southern Colleges and Courts and the Coming of the Civil War* (New York: Oxford University Press, 2016), 24.

2. See, e.g., David Brion Davis, *The Problem of Slavery in the Age of Emancipation* (New York: Knopf, 2014), 6–7.

3. John Quincy Adams, speech at Braintree, Massachusetts, September 17, 1842, quoted in *Memoir of the Life of John Quincy Adams*, by Josiah Quincy (Boston: Crosby, Nichols, & Lee, 1860), 385.

4. Robert Barnwell Rhett, "Speech at Grahamville, South Carolina, July 1859," in Rhett, *A Fire-Eater Remembers: The Confederate Memoir of Robert Barnwell Rhett*, ed. William C. Davis (Columbia: University of South Carolina Press, 2000), 7.

CHAPTER ONE: "Slavery Cannot Be Abolished"

1. John Jay to the president of the English Society for the Manumission of Slaves, June 1788, in *The Correspondence and Public Papers of John Jay*, ed. Henry P. Johnston, 4 vols. (New York: G. P. Putnam, 1893), 3:340; Rufus King to Timothy Pickering, November 4, 1803, in *The Life and Correspondence of Rufus King*, ed. Charles R. King, 6 vols. (New York: G. P. Putnam, 1900), 4:324. Hamilton and Burr, founders of the New York Manumission Society, both owned slaves.

2. Thomas Jefferson, *Notes on the State of Virginia* (London: Stockdale, 1787), 270, 364; Henry Wiencek, *An Imperfect God: George Washington, His Slaves, and the Creation of America* (New York: Farrar, Straus, & Giroux, 2003), 269; James Madison to Robert I. Evans, June 15, 1819, in *Writings of James Madison*, ed. Gaillard Hunt, 9 vols. (New York: Putnam, 1908), 8:439; Madison to James Madison Sr., September 8, 1783, ibid., 2:15; George Washington to David Stuart, March 28, 1790, in *The Writings of George Washington*, ed. John C. Fitzpatrick, 39 vols. (Washington DC: Government Printing Office, 1931–44), 31:28.

3. Richard S. Newman, "Prelude to the Gag-Rule: Southern Reaction to Antislavery Petitions in the First Federal Congress," *Journal of the Early Republic* 16 (1996): 577. The Three-Fifths Clause concerned the basis of representation in the House of

Representatives: "Representatives and direct Taxes shall be apportioned among the several States which may be included within this Union, according to their respective Numbers, which shall be determined by adding to the whole Number of free Persons, including those bound to Service for a Term of Years, and excluding Indians not taxed, three fifths of all other Persons" (article 1, section 2, paragraph 3, of the federal Constitution). The "other Persons" were slaves. Note that this implied that slaves were people, not property.

4. William Loughton Smith, speech in the House, March 17, 1790, *Annals of Congress*, 1st Cong., 2nd sess., 1503–4. On the Stono Rebellion in memory, see Peter Charles Hoffer, *Cry Liberty: The Great Stono River Slave Rebellion of 1739* (New York: Oxford University Press, 2010), 126–50.

5. Smith, Speech in the House, March 17, 1790, *Annals of Congress*, 1st Cong. 2nd sess., 1503–4.

6. William Maclay, quoted in Newman, "Prelude to the Gag-Rule," 587; final compromise, ibid., 591–95.

7. Henry Wiencek, *Master of the Mountain: Thomas Jefferson and His Slaves* (New York: Macmillan, 2013), 101; Carl E. Prince, "African Americans and the Constitutional Convention," in *Encyclopedia of African American History*, ed. Paul Finkelman, 3 vols. (New York: Oxford University Press, 2006), 2:343 (slavery would die of its own accord); Arthur Zilversmit, *The First Emancipation: The Abolition of Slavery in the North* (Chicago: University of Chicago Press, 1967); Gary John Kornblith, *Slavery and Sectional Strife in the Early American Republic, 1776–1821* (Lanham, MD: Rowman & Littlefield, 2007), 24–27; Adam Rothman, *Slave Country: American Expansion and the Origins of the Deep South* (Cambridge, MA: Harvard University Press, 2005), 26–27; Robert Pierce Forbes, *The Missouri Compromise and its Aftermath: Slavery and the Meaning of America*, 3rd ed. (Chapel Hill: University of North Carolina Press, 2007), 94–95. The concept of ripeness was introduced in another context by Felix Frankfurter. See *Communist Party of the United States v. Subversive Activities Control Board*, 367 U.S. 1, 501 (saying the issue was not ready for adjudication by the courts as there had not yet been an indictment).

8. "Yield nothing" quoted in Forbes, *Missouri Compromise*, 93; "a wolf by the ear" quoted from Thomas Jefferson to John Holmes, April 22, 1820, Thomas Jefferson Papers, Albert and Shirley Small Special Collections Library, University of Virginia Library, Charlottesville.

9. William Lee Miller, *Arguing about Slavery: John Quincy Adams and the Great Battle in the United States Congress* (New York: Knopf, 1996), 29. On resistance to abolitionist literature in the Deep South, see Lacy K. Ford, *Deliver Us from Evil: The Slavery Question in the Old South* (New York: Oxford University Press, 2009), 449–80. See, generally, Richard S. Newman, *The Transformation of American Abolitionism: Fighting Slavery in the Early Republic* (Chapel Hill: University of North Carolina Press, 2002), 131–75.

10. Henry Mayer, *All on Fire: William Lloyd Garrison and the Abolition of Slavery*

(New York: St. Martin's, 1998), 110–11; Newman, *Transformation of American Abolitionism*, 131; "An Appeal," *Liberator*, January 1, 1831.

11. Robert H. Abzug, *Passionate Liberator: Theodore Dwight Weld and the Dilemma of Reform* (New York: Oxford University Press, 1980), 82–85. The principal collaborators on the project were self-exiles from South Carolina, Sarah and Angelina Grimke. Gerda Lerner, *The Grimke Sisters from South Carolina*, rev. and expanded ed. (Chapel Hill: University of North Carolina Press, 2004), 101 and after.

12. *American Slavery As It Is: Testimony of A Thousand Witnesses* (New York: American Anti-Slavery Society, 1839), 7.

13. Newman, *Transformation of American Abolitionism*, 133.

14. Thomas M. Cooley, *A Treatise on the Constitutional Limitations . . .* (Boston: Little, Brown, 1868), 433.

15. Owen W. Muelder, *Theodore Dwight Weld and the American Anti-Slavery Society* (Jefferson, NC: McFarland, 2011), 38–39; Newman, "Prelude to the Gag-Rule," 571–99; National Postal Museum, "America's First Direct Mail Campaign," http://postalmuseumblog.si.edu/2010/07/americas-first-direct-mail-campaign.html.

16. Drew Gilpin Faust, *James Henry Hammond and the Old South: A Design for Mastery* (Baton Rouge: Louisiana State University Press, 1982), 179.

17. Miller, *Arguing about Slavery*, 140–49.

18. William Slade, speech in the House, December 16, 1835, *Register of Debates*, 24th Cong., 1st sess., 1962; James Henry Hammond, motion in the House, December 18, 1835, ibid., 1966.

19. Francis Thomas, speech in the House, December 18, 1835, ibid., 1972.

20. John Quincy Adams, speech in the House, December 21, 1835, ibid., 2000; Waddy Thompson, speech in the House, December 21, 1835, ibid., 2004; Henry A. Wise, speech in the House, December 22, 1835, ibid., 2032.

21. Slade, speech in the House, December 23, 1835, ibid., 2042.

22. Ibid., 2043.

23. Ibid.; William Stanton, *The Leopard's Spots: Scientific Attitudes toward Racism in America, 1815–1859* (Chicago: University of Chicago Press, 1960), documented the northern infatuation with racialist science; and George Frederickson, *The Inner Civil War: Northern Intellectuals and the Crisis of the Union*, rev. ed. (Urbana: University of Illinois Press, 1993), xiv, reminded readers that only a handful of northern reformers had sought equality for the freedmen.

24. Slade, speech in the House, 2043; ibid.; Leonard L. Richards, *Gentlemen of Property and Standing: Anti-Abolitionist Mobs in Jacksonian America* (New York: Oxford University Press, 1970), documents the provenance and policy of these mobs.

25. Richard Huzzey, *Freedom Burning: Anti-Slavery and Empire in Victorian Britain* (Ithaca, NY: Cornell University Press, 2012), 9–10 and after, documents the impact of the British legislation on American abolitionists.

26. Hammond, speech in the House, February 1, 1836, *Register of Debates*, 24th Cong., 2nd sess., 2453.

27. Ibid., 2450.

28. Ibid., 2451; see, e.g., Mark M. Smith, *Listening to Nineteenth-Century America* (Chapel Hill: University of North Carolina Press, 2001), 172–94.

29. Hammond, speech in the House, 2453. The patrol system is surveyed in Sally E. Hadden, *Slave Patrols: Law and Violence in Virginia and the Carolinas* (Cambridge, MA: Harvard University Press, 2001). The everyday forms of slaves' resistance are recounted in Kenneth Stampp, *The Peculiar Institution: Slavery in the Ante-Bellum South* (New York: Knopf, 1956). Accounts of slave rebellions are collected in Herbert Aptheker, *American Negro Slave Revolts* (New York: International, 1963). Individual slave rebellions are tracked in Hoffer, *Cry Liberty*; Hoffer, *The Great New York Slave Rebellion of 1741: Slavery, Crime, and Colonial Law* (Lawrence: University Press of Kansas, 2003); James Sidbury, *Ploughshares into Swords: Race, Rebellion, and Identity in Gabriel's Virginia, 1730–1810* (New York: Cambridge University Press, 1997); Daniel Rasmussen, *American Uprising: The Untold Story of America's Largest Slave Revolt* (New York: Harper, 2011); Douglas Edgerton, *He Shall Go Out Free: The Lives of Denmark Vesey* (Madison, WI: Madison House, 1999); and Stephen Oates, *The Fires of Jubilee: Nat Turner's Fierce Rebellion* (New York: Harper & Row, 1975).

30. Hammond, speech in the House, 2457.

31. Ibid., 2458; Frederick Merk, *Manifest Destiny and Mission in American History* (Cambridge, MA: Harvard University Press, 1963), 24–27; Ralph L. Ketcham, *The Political Thought of Benjamin Franklin* (Indianapolis: Bobbs-Merrill, 1965), xlviii–xlix.

32. Hammond, speech in the House, 2462.

33. Pinckney committee resolution, May 26, 1836, *Register of Debates*, 24th Cong., 1st sess., 4028.

34. *Richmond (VA) Enquirer*, May 31, 1836, 1.

35. John C. Calhoun, *A Disquisition on Government and Selections from the Discourse*, ed. C. Gordon Post (New York: Liberal Arts Press, 1953), 28.

36. John C. Calhoun, report of the Senate Select Committee on the Circulation of Incendiary Petitions, February 4, 1836, *Register of Debates*, 24th Cong., 2nd sess., appendix, 74.

37. The odd couple of American thought in this period was the new social science of sociology and the positive defense of slavery. Here Calhoun drew from and added to the work of Thomas B. Dew, a professor at William and Mary College, and a small circle of southern intellectuals and writers. Dorothy Ross, *The Origins of American Social Science* (New York: Cambridge University Press, 1992), 31–32.

38. Calhoun, report of the Senate Select Committee, 75. For critiques of this imposed chivalry, see Catherine Clinton, *The Plantation Mistress: Women's World in the Old South* (New York: Pantheon, 1982), 8 and after (the "oppression of women" of both races); and Stephanie McCurry, *Masters of Small Worlds: Yeoman Households, Gender Relations, and the Political Culture of the South Carolina Low Country* (New York: Oxford University Press, 1995). Male household heads imposed a kind of slavery on gender relations.

39. There is ample evidence for the market-oriented behavior of the master class.

See, e.g., James Oakes, *The Ruling Race: A History of American Slaveholders* (New York: Knopf, 1982). However, some historians still agree with Eugene Genovese, *The World the Slaveholders Made: Two Essays in Interpretation* (New York: Pantheon, 1969), which argues that the planters' market transactions did not change their premodern paternalistic view of themselves and their bondmen.

40. Calhoun, report of the Senate Select Committee, 76.

41. The argument for the comparative treatment of free industrial laborers and slave laborers was made in Robert William Fogel and Stanley L. Engerman, *Time on the Cross: The Economics of American Negro Slavery*, 2 vols. (New York: Norton, 1974), and in Herbert G. Guttman, *Slavery and the Numbers Game* (New York: Norton, 1975) and periodically thereafter. None of the participants in these scholarly exchanges exhibited the racism that Calhoun assumed.

42. Daniel Wirls, "'The Only Method of Avoiding Everlasting Debate': The Overlooked Senate Gag-Rule for Antislavery Petitions," *Journal of the Early Republic* 27 (2007): 115–38; James M. McPherson, "The Fight against the Gag-Rule: Joshua Leavitt and Antislavery Insurgency in the Whig Party, 1839–1842," *Journal of Negro History* 48 (1963): 177–95.

43. Kenneth I. Kersch, *Free Speech: Rights and Privileges under the Law* (Santa Barbara, CA: ABC-CLIO, 2003), 81; Thomas Hart Benton, quoted in *"The People's Darling Privilege": Struggles for Freedom of Expression in American History*, by Michael Kent Curtis (Durham, NC: Duke University Press, 2000), 141; AASS executive board, quoted in *The Slave's Cause: A History of Abolitionism*, by Manisha Sinha (New Haven, CT: Yale University Press, 2016), 250.

CHAPTER TWO: "Am I Gagged?"

1. John Quincy Adams, quoted in *The Scorpion's Sting: Antislavery and the Coming of the Civil War*, by James Oakes (New York: Norton, 2014), 137; Robert Remini, *John Quincy Adams* (New York: Times Books, 2002), 139–40 (Adams "despises" radical abolitionism); Leonard L. Richards, *The Life and Times of Congressman John Quincy Adams* (New York: Oxford University Press, 1988), 113 (Adams was motivated in part by political spite); David F. Ericson, "John Quincy Adams: Apostle of Union," in *A Companion to John Adams and John Quincy Adams*, ed. David Waldstreicher (New York: Wiley, 2013), 375–76 (evolution of his views from tolerating slavery to absolute opposition); Matthew Mason, "John Quincy Adams and the Tangled Politics of Slavery," in ibid., 402–21 (the impact of politics on Adams). On the *Antelope*, see Jonathan Bryant, *Dark Places of the Earth: The Voyage of the Slave Ship* Antelope (New York: Norton, 2015), 178.

2. John Quincy Adams, diary entry, August 11, 1835, in *Memoirs of John Quincy Adams*, ed. Charles Francis Adams, 12 vols. (Philadelphia: Lippincott, 1874–78), 9:252.

3. Adams, diary entry, December 26, 1835, ibid., 9:268.

4. Adams, diary entry, January 12, 1836, ibid., 9:271.

5. Adams, diary entry, May 26, 1836, ibid., 9:287.

6. John Quincy Adams, speech in the House, May 25, 1836, *Register of Debates*, 24th Cong., 1st sess., 4024, 4028.

7. Adams, diary entry, May 26, 1836, *Memoirs*, 9:286.

8. Adams, speech in the House, May 25, 1836, 4058, 4060; Adams, diary entry, May 26, 1836, *Memoirs*, 9:287, 288; Walter S. Franklin to James K. Polk, February 1836, in *Correspondence of James K. Polk*, ed. Herbert Weaver, 12 vols. (Nashville: Vanderbilt University Press, 1975), 3:663.

9. Adams, diary entry, July 27, 1836, *Memoirs*, 9:308; Adams, speech in the House, May 25, 1836, 4060. On the right to petition, see David C. Frederick, "John Quincy Adams, Slavery, and the Disappearance of the Right to Petition," *Law and History Review* 9 (1991): 114–21.

10. Adams, diary entry, July 9, 1836, *Memoirs*, 9:302.

11. *Southern Patriot* (Charleston, SC), April 14, 1836; Adams, diary entry, December 13, 1838, *Memoirs*, 10:63.

12. John Quincy Adams, speech in the House, December 26, 1836, *Register of Debates*, 24th Cong., 2nd sess., 1156–57.

13. Harry L. Watson, *Liberty and Power: The Politics of Jacksonian America* (New York: Hill & Wang, 1990), 73; Sean Wilentz, *The Rise of Democracy: Jefferson to Lincoln* (New York: Norton, 2005), 465.

14. Jon Meacham, *American Lion: Andrew Jackson in the White House* (New York: Random House, 2009), 165; Adams, diary entry, June 10, 1836, *Memoirs*, 9:295 (a southern editor attacks a northern editor in the gallery); Adams, diary entry, November 3, 1836, ibid., 9:311 (faint praise from another editor sparks Adams to note that "he has been one of the most virulent lampooners of me"); Adams, diary entry, February 4, 1842, ibid., 11:84–85 (accusing the *Globe* and the *Intelligencer* of misrepresenting him).

15. John Greenleaf Whittier, "Introductory Remarks," in *Letters from John Quincy Adams to His Constituents of the Twelfth Congressional District in Massachusetts. To which is added his speech in Congress, delivered February 9, 1837* (Boston: Knapp, 1837), 3; Adams, diary entry, October 28, 1836, *Memoirs*, 9:310. On Adams as a "man alone" in Congress, see Joseph Wheelan, *Mr. Adams' Last Crusade: John Quincy Adams' Extraordinary Post-Presidential Life in Congress* (New York: PublicAffairs, 2009), 81. Adams even wrote an essay titled *Lives of Celebrated Statesmen* (New York: Graham, 1846), focusing on James Madison, whose countenance, when looked at with a keen eye, much resembled the author's. What "duty" was due Madison by those who remembered him? he asked (41). It was to honor his sacrifices and his public service—"the still small voice that succeeded the whirlwind, the earthquake and the fire" (42). Surely the reference was to Adams's own voice as much as, or more than, Madison's.

16. Adams, *Letters from John Quincy Adams*, 7.

17. Ibid., 9.

18. Charles E. Haynes, speech in the House, February 6, 1837, *Register of Debates*, 24th Cong., 2nd sess., 1587. For the letter in question, see, e.g., The Petition of the Warriors of the Upper and Lower Sanduskies, October 6, 1806, presented to Con-

gress by Massachusetts Representative Joseph Varnum on December 22, 1806, and referred to Committee on Public Lands, https://research.archives.gov/id/306672.

19. Dixon Lewis, speech in the House, February 6, 1837, *Register of Debates*, 24th Cong., 2nd sess., 1588.

20. Ibid., 1587.

21. John Quincy Adams, speech in the House, February 6, 1837, ibid., 1587–88; Miller, *Arguing about Slavery*, 230–49; David Currie, *The Constitution in Congress: Descent into the Maelstrom, 1829–1861* (Chicago: University of Chicago Press, 2007), 20–21.

22. John Robertson, speech in the House, February 6, 1837, *Register of Debates*, 24th Cong., 2nd sess., 1614.

23. Martin Van Buren, Inaugural Address, March 4, 1837, in *Messages and Papers of the Presidents*, comp. James D. Richardson, vol. 4 (New York: Bureau of National Literature, 1989), 1530–32.

24. John Adams to George Churchman and Jacob Lindley, January 21, 1801, John Adams Papers, Massachusetts Historical Society, Boston.

25. Van Buren, Inaugural Address, 1533; Richard P. McCormick, *The Second Party System: Party Formation in the Jacksonian Era* (New York: Norton, 1966), 14–16 (the purpose of parties was to win the presidency).

26. Adams, diary entry, September 4, 1837, *Memoirs*, 9:366; John Seigenthaler, *James K. Polk* (New York: Times Books, 2004), 78; Charles Grier Sellers Jr., *James K. Polk, Jacksonian*, 2 vols. (Princeton, NJ: Princeton University Press, 1957), 1:339; Polk, diary entry, February 24, 1848, in *The Diary of James K. Polk during His Presidency, 1845 to 1849*, ed. Milo Milton Quaife, 4 vols. (Chicago: A. C. McClurg, 1910), 3:356.

27. Adams, diary entry, December 20, 1837, *Memoirs*, 9:453; Slade, speech in the House, December 18, 1837, *Congressional Globe*, 25th Cong., 1st sess., 30; Adams, diary entry, December 21, 1837, *Memoirs*, 9:454 (Adams thought that the clerk had not "disfigured and falsified the transactions"; Miller, *Arguing about Slavery*, 279–81.

28. Miller, *Arguing about Slavery*, 284–98; Adams, diary entry, December 21, 1837, *Memoirs*, 9:454.

29. Ibid., 304–6.

30. John C. Calhoun to John R. Mathewes, February 12, 1837, in *The Papers of John C. Calhoun*, ed. Robert L. Meriwether et al., 28 vols. (Columbia: University of South Carolina Press, 1959–75), 13:430.

CHAPTER THREE: "He Knew That They All Abhorred Slavery"

1. John W. Barber, *A History of the Amistad Captives . . . Also an Account of the Trials . . .* (New Haven, CT: Barber, 1840), 6; Peter Charles Hoffer, Williamjames Hull Hoffer, and N. E. H. Hull, *The Federal Courts: An Essential History* (New York: Oxford University Press, 2016), 127–29.

2. Howard Jones, *Mutiny on the* Amistad (New York: Oxford University Press, 1988); Bruce A. Ragsdale, "'Incited by the Love of Liberty': The *Amistad* Captives and

the Federal Courts," *Prologue* 35 (2003), http://www.archives.gov/publications/pro
logue/2003/spring/amistad-2.html. Both district courts, over which a single district
judge presided, and circuit courts, over which a justice of the Supreme Court assigned
to that judicial circuit and the district court judge jointly presided, were trial courts.

3. Miller, *Arguing about Slavery*, 145.

4. Roger Baldwin, counsel for appellants in error, "Prior History," 61, *United States
v. Claimants of Schooner Amistad*, 40 U.S. 518 (1841).

5. *United States v. Libellants and Claimants of the Schooner Amistad*, 40 U.S. 518; Ted
Widmer, *Martin Van Buren* (New York: Macmillan, 2006), 121–22.

6. John Quincy Adams, *Argument of John Quincy Adams, before the Supreme Court
of the United States: in the case of the United States, appellants, vs. Cinque, and others,
Africans, captured in the schooner Amistad, by Lieut. Gedney, delivered on the 24th of
February and 1st of March, 1841. With a review of the case of the Antelope, reported in the
10th, 11th, and 12th volumes of Wheaton's Reports* (New York: S. W. Benedict, 1841), 3.

7. Ibid., 4; Remini, *John Quincy Adams*, 147; Eric Foner, *Free Soil, Free Labor, Free
Men: The Ideology of the Republican Party before the Civil War*, rev. ed. (New York:
Oxford University Press, 1995), 150. Van Buren's turn to the free-soil cause owed as
much to southern opposition to his presidential renomination in 1844 as to Adams's
dislike of Van Buren. Adams's dislike of Van Buren, in similar fashion, was partly ow-
ing to Van Buren's role in Adams's defeat in 1828.

8. Adams, *Argument before the Supreme Court*, 4.

9. Ibid., 9; Rick Dyson, "The Amistad Case," in *Encyclopedia of Slave Resistance
and Rebellion*, ed. Junius P. Rodriguez, 2 vols. (Westport, CT: Greenwood, 2007), 1:19.

10. Adams, *Argument before the Supreme Court*, 21.

11. Ibid., 39.

12. Ibid., 43.

13. Ibid., 87.

14. Ibid., 88.

15. Joshua Giddings, "The Trial and Triumph of John Quincy Adams, in 1842,"
lecture to the New York Anti-Slavery Society, December 5, 1854, reprinted in *National
Anti-Slavery Standard*, December 16, 1854.

16. Miller, *Arguing about Slavery*, 433–34; *Congressional Globe*, 27th Cong., 2nd
sess. 89–90, 168–69 (1842).

17. Adams, diary entry, June 4, 1838, *Memoirs*, 10:8–9; Giddings, "Trial and Triumph of John Quincy Adams"; Wheelan, *Mr. Adams' Last Crusade*, 198–202.

18. Giddings, "Trial and Triumph of John Quincy Adams"; George Washington
Julian, *Life of Joshua R. Giddings* (Chicago: McClurg, 1892), 104–10.

19. Giddings, "Trial and Triumph of John Quincy Adams."

20. Comte de Buffon, quoted in *Romantic Medicine and John Keats*, by Hermione
de Almeida (New York: Oxford University Press, 1990), 55. On phrenology, the popular source at the time was George Combe, *A System of Phrenology* (Boston: Mussey,
1851). On Adams and phrenology, see John Quincy Adams to Dr. Sewall, April 5, 1839,
reprinted in Combe, *Notes on the United States of America: During a Phrenological Visit*

in 1838–9–40, 2 vols. (Boston, 1841), 2:376; Giddings, "Trial and Triumph of John Quincy Adams."

21. Adams, diary entry, January 26, 1842, *Memoirs*, 11:74; *Congressional Globe*, 27th Cong., 2nd sess., 186–89 (1842).

22. Ibid., 189–91, 200–201. On Athenian democracy in the rhetoric of antebellum southern politics, see James C. Cobb, *Away Down South: A History of Southern Identity* (New York: Oxford University Press, 2005), 42.

23. Adams, diary entry, March 7, 1838, *Memoirs*, 9:503. See also Giddings, "Trial and Triumph of John Quincy Adams."

24. *Congressional Globe*, 27th Cong., 2nd sess., 192 (indistinct remarks); Miller, *Arguing about Slavery*, 443 (death threats).

25. John Quincy Adams, speech in the House, February 3, 1842, *Congressional Globe*, 27th Cong., 2nd sess., 203–8.

26. Joseph P. Ellis, *Founding Brothers: The Revolutionary Generation* (New York: Knopf, 2003), 114 (Madison); Wiencek, *Master of the Mountain*, 27 (Jefferson denounces slavery in *Notes on the State of Virginia*); Philip J. Schwarz, *Slavery at the Home of George Washington* (Charlottesville: University of Virginia Press, 2002), 143 (Washington's will frees his slaves upon the passing of Martha).

27. Adams, diary entry, December 3, 1844, *Memoirs*, 12:115, 116, 479–80; James Henry Hammond, diary entry, December 22, 1844, in *Secret and Sacred: The Diaries of James Henry Hammond, a Southern Slaveholder*, ed. Carol K. Bleser (New York: Oxford University Press, 1988), 138.

28. Wirls, "Avoiding Everlasting Debate," 134.

29. Adams, diary entries, December 19, 28, 1844, *Memoirs*, 12:93, 133.

CHAPTER FOUR: "How Can the Union Be Preserved?"

1. Edmund Ruffin, *The Political Economic of Slavery* (Washington DC: Towers, 1853), 3–4; Robert Toombs to the Few Literary Society, Emory College, Georgia, 1853, quoted in Brophy, *University, Court, and Slave*, 102.

2. See, generally, Frederick Merk, *Slavery and the Annexation of Texas* (New York: Knopf, 1972).

3. Fred Kaplan, *John Quincy Adams: American Visionary* (New York: Harper, 2014), 563; David Wilmot, speech in the House, February 8, 1847, *Congressional Globe*, 29th Cong., 2nd sess., appendix, 16318; Calhoun, speech in the Senate, February 19, 1847, ibid., 453, 455.

4. Robert V. Remini, *Henry Clay: Statesman for the Union* (New York: Norton, 1992), 730–61; Merrill D. Peterson, *The Great Triumvirate: Webster, Clay, and Calhoun* (New York: Oxford University Press, 1987), 449–75.

5. Peterson, *Great Triumvirate*, 452; Michael S. Green, *Politics and America in Crisis: The Coming of the Civil War* (Santa Barbara, CA: ABC-CLIO, 2010), 35.

6. Calhoun, speech in the Senate, March 4, 1850, *Congressional Globe*, 31st Cong., 1st sess., 451.

7. Ibid., 451. On the classical style of oratory in the age of Calhoun and Lincoln, see Garry Wills, *Lincoln at Gettysburg: The Words That Remade America* (New York: Simon & Schuster, 1992).

8. Calhoun, speech in the Senate, March 4, 1850, 452.

9. Ibid., 453.

10. James Madison, Federalist No. 10, November 22, 1787 (parties and interests prevented from seizing control of the nation); Federalist No. 51, February 6, 1788 (checks and balances system).

11. Gregory Leyh, *Legal Hermeneutics: History, Theory, and Practice* (Berkeley: University of California Press, 1992), 87; Hammond, speech in the Senate, March 4, 1858, *Congressional Globe*, 35th Cong., 1st sess., 960.

12. Calhoun, speech in the Senate, March 4, 1850, 453–54.

13. Ibid., 455. See, e.g., William W. Freehling, *Prelude to Civil War: The Nullification Controversy in South Carolina, 1816–1836* (New York: Oxford University Press, 1965), 153–58 (Calhoun's shift from nationalism to nullification); and Peterson, *Great Triumvirate*, 252–64 (how abolition becomes Calhoun's great fear).

14. Calhoun, speech in the Senate, 455.

15. Ibid.; Eric Foner, *Free Soil, Free Labor, Free Men*, 11–39.

16. Diana Fuss, "Last Words," *ELH* 76 (2009): 877–910; Calhoun, speech in the Senate, 455.

17. Calhoun, speech in the Senate, 455. See, e.g., Stanley W. Campbell, *The Slave Catchers: Enforcement of the Fugitive Slave Law, 1850–1860* (Chapel Hill: University of North Carolina Press, 2012), 148–86. Richard Hofstadter, *American Political Tradition* (New York: Knopf, 1948), 91, suggests that Calhoun had "a certain perversity of mind" that blinded him to the weakness of a slave South. Certainly it did not blind him to the likelihood that the leaders of that section would rather go to war than surrender any of their property.

18. Robert V. Remini, *Daniel Webster: The Man and His Time* (New York: Norton, 1997), 67–68, 145–46, 176, 177, 464.

19. Wirls, "Avoiding Everlasting Debate," 127.

20. Daniel Webster, speech in the Senate, March 7, 1850, *Congressional Globe*, 31st Cong., 1st sess., 476.

21. Thomas D. Morris, *Freemen All: The Personal Liberty Laws of the North, 1780–1861* (Baltimore: Johns Hopkins University Press, 1974), 135; Remini, *Daniel Webster*, 673.

22. Webster, speech in the Senate, 476; Remini, *Daniel Webster*, 28.

23. Webster, speech in the Senate, 476.

24. See, e.g., Paul Finkelman, *Slavery and the Founders: Race and Liberty in the Age of Jefferson*, 3rd ed. (Armonk, NY: M. E. Sharpe, 2014), 94–95; Webster, speech in the Senate, 477.

25. Eugene Genovese, *A Consuming Fire: The Fall of the Confederacy in the Mind of the White Christian South* (Athens: University of Georgia Press, 1999), 1–34; Christine Heyrman, *Southern Cross: The Beginnings of the Bible Belt* (Chapel Hill: University of North Carolina Press, 1998), 206–52.

26. See, e.g., John R. McKivigan, "The Sectional Division of the Methodist and Baptist Denominations as Measures of Northern Antislavery Sentiment," in *Religion and the Antebellum Debate over Slavery*, ed. McKivigan and Mitchell Snay (Athens: University of Georgia Press, 1998), 343–64.

27. Webster, speech in the Senate, 477.

28. See, e.g., Earl Maltz, *Fugitive Slave on Trial: The Anthony Burns Case and Abolitionist Outrage* (Lawrence: University Press of Kansas, 2010).

29. Webster, speech in the Senate, 478.

30. *Prigg v. Pennsylvania*, 41 U.S. 539 (1842).

31. Webster, speech in the Senate, 481. The much-awarded movie and book *Twelve Years a Slave* dramatize Solomon Northrup's kidnapping and enslavement. It was a not uncommon event. The book, *Twelve Years A Slave: A True Story of Betrayal, Kidnap, and Slavery*, was originally published in 1853; a reprint edition was published in London by Hesperus in 2013. The movie appeared in 2013.

32. Webster, speech in the Senate, 482. These comments led to a widespread campaign of vilification of Webster in the free states. He was regarded as an apostate from the cause of antislavery. His former friends in the antislavery movement were shocked, saddened, and infuriated, accusing Webser of cold-heartedness and expediency. See, e.g., James B. Stewart, "Heroes, Villains, Liberty, and License: The Abolitionist Vision of Wendell Phillips," in *Antislavery Reconsidered: New Perspectives on the Abolitionists*, ed. Lewis Perry and Michael Fellman (Baton Rouge: Louisiana State University Press, 1979), 185; and David Grant, *Political Antislavery Discourse and American Literature of the 1850s* (Newark: University of Delaware Press, 2012), 27–28.

33. Webster, speech in the Senate, 482.

34. Nat Turner's Rebellion (August 21–23, 1831), on the south side of the James River, resulted in the murder of more than fifty whites and the execution of more than one hundred slaves. Patrick H. Breen, *The Land Shall Be Deluged in Blood: A New History of the Nat Turner Revolt* (New York: Oxford University Press, 2015), 31–98.

35. Webster, speech in the Senate, 482.

36. James M. McPherson, *For Cause and Comrades: Why Men Fought in the Civil War* (New York: Oxford University Press, 1997), 30–31; James Longstreet, *From Manassas to Appomattox: Memoirs of the Civil War in America*, 2nd ed., rev. (Philadelphia: J. B. Lippincott, 1908), vi; Webster, speech in the Senate, 482.

37. Webster, speech in the Senate, 482–83. On changing concepts of marriage and divorce in this period, see Hendrik Hartog, *Man and Wife in America: A History* (Cambridge, MA: Harvard University Press, 2000), 108–13.

38. Calhoun to Andrew Jackson, June 1, 1820, in *The Papers of John C. Calhoun*, 5:165.

39. Rhett, quoted in *Rhett: The Turbulent Life and Times of a Fire-Eater*, ed. William C. Davis (Columbia: University of South Carolina Press, 2001), 283; Webster, speech in the Senate, 483.

40. Webster, speech in the Senate, 483; Gordon Wood, *The Radicalism of the*

American Revolution (New York: Knopf, 1991), 104 (founders and civic virtue), 217 (middle-period shift away from public virtue); Webster, speech in the Senate, 483.

41. On the reception of Webster's speech, see Holman Hamilton, *Prologue to Conflict: The Crisis and Compromise of 1850* (Lexington: University Press of Kentucky, 2015), 79–80; on the oratory of Clay, Webster, and Calhoun, see Peterson, *Great Triumvirate*, 33, 107, 382. One might cite exceptions to this generalization—Charles Sumner of Massachusetts, for example, could speak for days, and did, against the Kansas-Nebraska Act of 1854.

Epilogue

1. Theodore Dwight Weld, quoted in *Theodore Dwight Weld: A Biography*, by Robert Henry Abzug, 2 vols. (Berkeley: University of California Press, 1977), 2:337. The Kansas-Nebraska Act opened Kansas's petition for statehood to a popular referendum. Slave supporters and Free-Soilers rushed into the territory from Missouri and Iowa. The result was a series of bloody confrontations and a slave constitution that antislavery members of Congress could not swallow. The issue continued to enflame Congress until the Civil War erupted, after which Kansas was admitted as a free state.

2. Adams, diary entry, December 13, 1838, *Memoirs*, 10:63.

3. William Henry Seward, speech in Rochester, New York, October 25, 1858, in *The Works of William H. Seward*, ed. George E. Baker, 5 vols. (Boston: Houghton Mifflin, 1884), 4:295.

4. James M. Buchanan, speech in Wheatland, Pennsylvania, October 1860, on the occasion of his nomination as the Democratic presidential candidate, quoted in *Life of James Buchanan*, by George Ticknor Curtis, 2 vols. (New York: Harper, 1883), 2:175; David F. Jamison, "South Carolina," in *American Annual Cyclopedia . . . for the Year 1861* (1867), quoted in *Liberty and Union: The Civil War Era and American Constitutionalism*, by Timothy S. Huebner (Lawrence: University Press of Kansas, 2016), 117.

5. Eric Foner, *The Fiery Trial: Abraham Lincoln and American Slavery* (New York: Norton, 2010), 189–92; Alexander Tsesis, *The Thirteenth Amendment: A Legal History* (New York: New York University Press, 2004), 35–39.

ESSAY ON SOURCES

Listening to the past is the focus of Mark M. Smith, *Listening to Nineteenth-Century America* (Chapel Hill: University of North Carolina Press, 2001). It is part of an effort of many scholars to re-create the "soundscape" of the past and bring it to life once again. How people heard was regional; that is, their experiences at home influenced how they heard noises, voices, and sound when they traveled. One full-dress scholarly account of the gag-rule debates in Congress is available. William Lee Miller's quasi-journalistic, "you are there" account, *Arguing about Slavery: John Quincy Adams and the Great Battle in the United States Congress* (New York: Knopf, 1996), is long (almost 600 pages) and replete with moral judgments, sharp rebukes, heroes and villains, and the triumph of good (Adams) over evil (just about every southern politician), but well worth reading. Miller does not overstate Adams's role in the story, but he may exaggerate the importance of the gag-rule debates in Adams's career in Congress. Adams spent as much time on foreign affairs (after all, he was a former secretary of state and diplomat) and the admission of Texas (which he opposed) as he did on the question of the antislavery petition's reception. Given the importance of the gag-rule debates, one wonders why there are not many more books devoted to the subject.

A handful of scholarly articles are devoted to the debate. See, for example, Michael Kent Curtis, "The Curious History of Attempts to Suppress Antislavery Speech, Press, and Petition in 1835–1837," *Northwestern Law Review* 89 (1995): 785–849; David C. Frederick, "John Quincy Adams, Slavery, and the Disappearance of the Right to Petition," *Law and History Review* 9 (1991): 113–55; James M. McPherson, "The Fight against the Gag-Rule: Joshua Leavitt and Antislavery Insurgency in the Whig Party, 1839–1842," *Journal of Negro History* 48 (1963): 177–95; Scott R. Meinke, "Slavery, Partisanship, and Procedure in the U.S. House," *Legislative Studies Quarterly* 32 (2007): 33–57; Richard S. Newman, "Prelude to the Gag-Rule: Southern Reaction to Antislavery Petitions in the First Federal Congress," *Journal of the Early Republic* 16 (1996): 571–99; George C. Rable, "Slavery, Politics, and the South: The Gag-Rule as a Case Study," *Capitol Studies* 3 (1975): 69–87; Gordon M. Weiner, "Pennsylvania Congressmen and the 1836 Gag Rule: A Quantitative Note," *Pennsylvania History* 36 (1959): 335–40; and Daniel Wirls, " 'The Only Mode of Avoiding Everlasting Debate': The Overlooked Senate Gag-Rule for Antislavery Petitions," *Journal of the Early Republic* 27 (2007): 115–38.

There are also a few websites devoted to the gag rule. They include http://www.archives.gov/exhibits/treasures_of_congress/text/page10_text.html; http://history

.house.gov/Historical-Highlights/1800-1850/The-House-of-Representatives-insti tuted-the-%E2%80%9Cgag-rule%E2%80%9D/; http://www.pbs.org/wnet/slavery /experience/freedom/docs3.html; and http://www.digitalhistory.uh.edu/disp_text book.cfm?smtID=3&psid=376. One should use them with care, as websites tend to have a particular "take" on the subject or omit important details.

Just about every biographer of Adams accords his part in the debate some space. Samuel Flagg Bemis, *John Quincy Adams and the Union* (New York: Knopf, 1956), 370, found Adams an abolitionist at heart, while Leonard L. Richards, *The Life and Times of Congressman John Quincy Adams* (New York: Oxford University Press, 1988), 113–203, opined that Adams's opposition to the gag rule was a form of revenge against the Jacksonian Democrats, who had cost him his reelection. According to Harlow Gates Unger, *John Quincy Adams* (Boston: Da Capo, 2012), 274, Adams "all but exploded with rage" when he found he was gagged. Fred Kaplan, *John Quincy Adams: American Visionary* (New York: Harper, 2014), 507, wrote that "with a gift for the melodrama of high patriotism, he merged the power of who he was with the power of his message." Robert V. Remini, *John Quincy Adams* (New York: Times Books, 2002), 140, concluded that "Adams led the fight." Paul C. Nagel, *John Quincy Adams: A Public Life, a Private Life* (New York: Knopf, 1997), 361, waxed eloquent about Adams, writing that "glorying in his skill at taunting and outfoxing his enemies," Adams found ways to bring up the subject of the petitions despite the gag. In a segment of the C-SPAN show *Booknotes*, Nagel claimed that Adams was the "sole champion" of freedom of speech in the gag-rule debates, a judgment that is somewhat unfair to other antislavery proponents. Nagel appeared on the show on January 4, 1998, and the interview is available at http://www.booknotes.org/Watch/94696-1/Paul+Nagel.aspx. David Waldstreicher edited *A Companion to John Adams and John Quincy Adams* (New York: Wiley, 2013) for the Blackwell Companions series; it is available online as well as in print. In it, Waldstreicher, "John Quincy Adams: Life Biographers, Diary," 254–57, assesses other historians' views of Adams's role in the debates, as does Matthew Mason, "John Quincy Adams and the Tangled Politics of Slavery," 403–4.

Relatively brief mention of the debates appears in other secondary sources on slavery, abolition, and the antebellum Congresses, as well as in biographies of the other principals. References to these appear in the notes to this volume. In addition, there are short entries in a variety of encyclopedias. See, for example, Jesse Kratz, "Gag-rule," in *Encyclopedia of United States Congress*, ed. Robert E. Dewhirst and John David Raucsch (New York: Infobase, 2009), 227–28; Junius P. Rodriguez, "Gag Resolution," in *Encyclopedia of Manumission and Abolition in the Transatlantic World*, ed. Rodriguez (New York: Routledge, 2015), 241–42; Stephen W. Stathis, "House Gag-Rule, 1836–1844," in *Landmark Debates in Congress*, ed. Stathis (Washington DC: CQ Press, 2009), 109–18; and William L. Richter, "Gag Rule," in *Historical Dictionary of the Old South* (Lanham, MD: Scarecrow, 2006), 159–60.

It is not hard to find the primary sources for the debates. Joseph Gales Jr. and William Winston Seaton's *Register of Debates in Congress* and Francis Preston Blair and John C. Rives's somewhat less helpful *Congressional Globe* are online at the Library of

Congress's American Memory, a Century of Lawmaking website, https://memory.loc
.gov/ammem/amlaw/lawhome.html. Printed copies can be found in the government-
documents section of major research libraries designated government-document re-
positories. Such libraries receive free copies from the Government Printing Office
and in turn must allow the public free access to them. The full reference for the
Register of Debates is *Register of Debates in Congress, Comprising the Leading Debates and
Incidents of the Second Session of the 18th Congress [December 6, 1824 to First Session of
the 25th Congress, October 16, 1837], Together with an Appendix Containing the Most Important State Papers and Public Documents to which the Session has given Birth; to which
are Added the Laws Enacted during the Session, with a Copious Index to the Whole* (Washington DC: Gales & Seaton, 1825–37). The catalog reference for the *Globe* is United
States Congress, *Congressional Globe . . . [23d Congress to the 42d Congress, December 2,
1833, to March 3, 1873]* (Washington DC: various publishers).

The debates in the *Register* and the *Globe* have to be read with some caution. The
publisher of the *Register* promised a summary of "the leading debates and incidents"
covering the period 1824–37 "to supply a deficiency in our political annals . . . the history of legislation of the government of the United States." In short, the original purpose was to track the course of motions, resolutions, and bills through both houses,
not to present a verbatim record. The "Preface" to the first volume of the *Register* con-
cedes that "these debates in all cases are not literally reported, but their substantial
accuracy may be entirely relied upon." Reporters tried to take notes, but most of the
long speeches printed in the record were only approximations of what was said at the
time. When members wanted readers to have a full, sometimes emended version of a
speech, they gave reporters a copy. The *Globe*, also a private publication, overlapped
the *Register* for the years 1833–37, then continued through 1873, when it was replaced
by the Government Printing Office's own *Congressional Record*. The *Globe*'s coverage
comprised condensed reports until 1851, with reporters on occasion even noting that
they could not follow what members were saying. After that time, it more closely ap-
proximated a verbatim account.

Newspapers, especially Hezekiah Niles's Baltimore-based *Weekly Register*, carried
accounts of debates in Congress until the demise of the editor, and with him the
newspaper, in 1839. Although the paper was devoted to political topics, Niles did not
adhere to one of the major political parties. He was not a defender of slavery, however, and thus incurred the wrath of those who were. Although the paper focused on
the Washington DC area, Niles included squibs from other newspapers, including
those in Richmond and Charleston. James Gordon Bennett's sensationalist *New-York
Herald* (1835–1924) was more typical of the mass-circulation papers of the time. It
featured lurid tales of crime and corruption. Bennett, unlike Niles, was a partisan,
and favored Whig candidates. He had no love for abolitionists. Bennett had reporters in the gallery of the House during the gag-rule debates. The *Charleston Mercury*
was founded in 1819 by Henry L. Pinckney, a name familiar to students of the gag
rule. Pinckney ran the *Mercury* until 1834 and served in Congress from 1833 to 1837.
William Lloyd Garrison's *Liberator* (1831–65) continued publication through the war.

Its stance on the gag rule was the opposite of the *Mercury*'s. Although Garrison's paper had relatively few subscribers, it was widely influential. It followed the gag-rule debates closely. Issues of papers covering the gag rule are available online at fair-use .org; at Readex's American Historical Newspapers, http://www.readex.com/content /americas-historical-newspapers; and at the Library of Congress local-newspapers archive, https://www.loc.gov/rr/news/oltitles.html.

The letters and diary of John Quincy Adams are available at the Massachusetts Historical Society website, http://www.masshist.org/jqadiaries/php/. There one finds scanned images of the handwritten originals; earlier the society sold microfilms of the papers. William Peden and Adrienne Koch published a selection of the writings of John and John Quincy Adams in 1946. Allen Nevins published a selection from the diaries in 1929. The standard, full print edition of the diaries is *The Memoirs of John Quincy Adams*, edited by John Quincy Adams's son Charles Francis Adams, 12 vols. (Philadelphia: J. B. Lippincott, 1874–77). The standard collection of John C. Calhoun's writings is *The Papers of John C. Calhoun*, ed. Robert L. Meriwether et al., 28 vols. (Columbia: University of South Carolina Press, 1959–75). And Webster's papers are being published as *The Papers of Daniel Webster*, ed. Charles M. Wiltse et al., 8 vols. to date (Hanover, NH: University Press of New England, 1974–).

INDEX

Page numbers in *italics* indicate images.

abolition of slavery: and characterizations of abolitionists, 5, 18–19, 24, 31, 37, 72, 80; and destruction of abolitionist materials, 14–15, 25; and dissolution of Union, threats of, 22–23; and gradualism, 19–20; John Adams on, 40; John Quincy Adams on, 29, 31, 87; and mail campaigns, 13–15, 80; morality of, 22; Northern disagreement on, 33; and Quakers, 2–3, 7–9; and religiosity, 77; and use of press, 10–13, 21; and vilification of Webster, 99n32; violence against, 10, 14–15, 20, 25, 27, 35; and Virginia, 2–3. *See also* petitions for abolition of slavery

Adams, John, 40

Adams, John Quincy, *30*, *62*; on abolition / end of slavery, 29, 31, 32–33, 87; and *Amistad* case, 45, 46–53; and annexation of Texas, 62, 65; calls to censure, 36–39, 52, 53–61; career of, 1–2, 5, 28–29, 35–36, 74; character of, 1–2, 28, 51, 60; death of, 62, *62*; on duty, 36, 94n15; on slavery, 1, 3, 29; as speaker, 32, 60, 67; Whig Party role of, 1, 30. *See also* gag rule; petitions for abolition of slavery

American Anti-Slavery Society, 10–13, 21, 27

American Colonization Society, 10

American Slavery As It Is (Weld), 11–13

Amistad (ship), 45–53

Antelope (ship), 28–29

antikidnapping laws, 79

appearance, conflation with character, 57, 75

apprenticeship, 20

Baldwin, Roger, 48, 49

Benton, Thomas Hart, 27

black codes, 77

Brown, John, 85

Buchanan, James, 88

Butler, Andrew Pickens, 66

Calhoun, John C., *68*; and *Amistad*, 51; career of, 24, 73–74; and Compromise of 1850, 63, 65–73; death of, 72; and defense of slavery, 24–27, 71–73, 92n37, 98n17; and gag rule, 27, 67–68; on Missouri Compromise, 82–83; and nullification, 24–25, 33; as speaker, 67; on unifying South, 43, 83

California and Compromise of 1850, 4, 65–67

censure, calls to, 36–39, 52, 53–61

character, conflation with appearance, 57, 75

chivalry, imposed, 25–26, 92n38

Cilley, Jonathan, 59

Clay, Henry, 66

colonies, British, 20, 29

colonization of slaves, 10

Combe, George, 57

Committee on the District, 17

Compromise of 1850: Calhoun, 63, 65–73; and centrality of slavery debate, 4; as respite, 88; and Webster, 63, 65, 73–85

concurrent majority, 24

Constitution: and *Federalist Papers*, 68–69, 70; slavery in, 7, 36, 40, 52, 89–90n3; as theme in gag-rule debates, 5

Constitutional Convention, 40

Cooper, Mark, 58

cotton industry, 9–10, 69, 75

court jurisdiction, 46, 95–96n2

Cuba and *Amistad* case, 45–53